THE RENEGADE GIRLS TINKERING CLUB

THE RENEGADE SUCCESS PLAN

Terri Selting David

Copyright © 2021 by Terri Selting David

ISBN: 978-1-7354545-6-6

All rights reserved.

No part of this book may be reproduced in any form or by any electronic or mechanical means, including information storage and retrieval systems, without written permission from the author, except for the use of brief quotations in a book review.

This book is a work of fiction. Names, characters, business, events and incidents are the products of the author's imagination. Any resemblance to actual persons, living or dead, or actual events is coincidental, or at most, inspirational. The science, however, and amazing women from history are all real and important.

*To Dad, who always supports
my crazy business schemes.*

This one is for you.

1

WARM-UP

"Career Week!" Benjamin Spencer's eyes glowed with excitement. "It's gonna be big. I need all the help I can get, and can't think of anyone better to ask than you and the other Renegades."

"I really don't have time to talk right now," Ivy Rose Park passed her basketball to the girl on her right. "Kind of in the middle of something."

Ada Lovelace Charter School's gym echoed with the sounds of practice as the girls on Ivy's team dribbled through their drills. Sneakers squeaked on the glossy wood court floor, punctuated by the occasional grunt or coach's whistle. Water dripped from a wet Benjamin in tiny splashes, pooling at his feet as he waited on the sidelines for a more satisfactory reply from Ivy.

She hesitated. She liked Benjamin. He'd done a lot for the school. Captain of the swim team (he was supposed to be at practice with them right now), president of student council, winning trophy after trophy with the now marginally more popular competitive math team. On top of all that, he was also a really nice guy.

And he was her friend.

But Ivy was here to improve her game. To be the best, you had to have focus. If she was going to be an electrical engineer and run her own company someday, she had to learn how to succeed. How to win. How to achieve her goals. And right now her goal was to help the Lovelace Machines have a good season. Her responsibility right now was to them. They were her team and she couldn't let anything stand in her way. Not even Benjamin.

Who was, literally, standing in her way right now.

She craned her neck around him, trying to see which drill her teammates were setting up. A few steps away Emma Bloom crouched near an orange cone, watching her impatiently.

"Park!" yelled Coach Bakes. "Social time later. Bloom's waiting for you. Spencer, you get back to your swim practice. And clean up that water before somebody slips on it and breaks their neck!"

"Sorry Coach Bakes!" Benjamin saluted her with a grin, as if they were sharing some kind of a joke. He pulled the towel from his shoulders and patted at the water pooling under his feet. "I've been trying to talk to Ivy here for days. I'm lucky she had practice today, too, or I might never have pegged her down."

"I don't care if you're donating a kidney to her, get

yourself back to your own practice and let my girls concentrate."

Benjamin turned back to Ivy. And waited.

Ivy glanced at her coach, then at Emma, then back at Benjamin.

Practice was already running late and she certainly couldn't afford to make it later. Not today. She had to get rid of Benjamin, but in as nice a way as possible.

"Look," she said in desperation, "if I promise we'll help you, can we talk about it later?"

"Awesome! I'll find you guys at lunch on Monday. It's my last event as president before I head off to high school, and I really want to make a splash, no pun intended."

He nudged Ivy with a wink that said the pun was very much intended and headed back through the glass doors that separated the pool from the basketball court.

Ivy turned back to the drill.

A second orange cone waited halfway across the gym. Nearby, Emma shifted her weight from foot to foot like a cat waiting to pounce. It was go time.

"3... 2... 1... GO!"

Ivy took off, dribbling with her left hand. Emma took off after her.

Ivy wobbled. Just a bit.

Dribbling with her left hand was awkward, but that was the whole point of the drill. To work on her weaknesses.

Weaknesses.

She had just added yet another time commitment to

her plate. And she'd have to tell the others in the Renegade Girls Tinkering Club that she'd volunteered them all. How was she going to fit in another obligation between basketball, the tinkering club, homework, and the online electronics class she'd signed up for after school? At least the class was just a refresher on the basics of electricity, pretty simple stuff. For her anyway.

Growing up with an electrical engineer for a mother, Ivy learned about electricity and circuits from her earliest board books. *Baby's First Circuit* had been a joke gift. It wasn't really intended to teach an infant how to rewire a computer. But it was probably why Ivy had always associated volts, currents, and amperage with cuddling up in her mom's warm lap. It had always been just her and her mom. And her mom's job.

So, time spent learning about her mom's passion was precious time spent with her mom. Now, Ivy saw the whole world moving around like electricity through a circuit board. She liked to imagine the current flowed through her, too, as if she were a circuit herself.

As Ivy rounded the far cone and headed for the basket, she imagined brilliant white electrical energy spark out from her core, zapping around her shoulder, flowing through the angle of her elbow, speeding to her hand, and surrounding the ball. She transitioned smoothly into a layup as Emma reached out to block her shot.

With an expert flick of her wrist, Ivy released the crackling energy. It was almost real to her, this line of power trailing behind the ball as it soared towards the basket, passing right over Emma's reaching hands. The electric tail curved along the path it traveled, its trajectory, in a graceful, almost perfect arc.

Almost.

The ball smacked into the backboard — and bounced right off. A brick shot.

Ivy groaned.

Emma caught the ball on the rebound, dribbled twice, and passed it back to Ivy as they jogged to the start to try again.

By the time practice finished, Ivy's shirt dripped with sweat. Salty sweat might be a good conductor of electricity, but right now it was just the stinky cost of getting better.

In the locker room, Emma and her other teammates giggled and gossiped as they changed. They were going to grab some pizza together, but Ivy couldn't join them. Not today.

She waved quickly and rushed out the door. She'd given the practice her all. It was time to switch priorities.

"See you tomorrow at the game!" yelled Emma. "We're gonna—"

The door shut off her words like a switch. Ivy's mother was already waiting at the curb out front.

Mom hated waiting.

"You don't have much time, honey," her mom said as Ivy slid into the passenger seat.

"I know. Sorry." Ivy flopped her gym bag on the car floor. "Practice ran into overtime. I came out as fast as I could."

Her mom nodded as she pulled into traffic. "By the way, your new book came in. It's there on the dash."

"REALLY?!" Ivy squealed. She tore open the package and extracted the book.

Success Plan by Dr. Caroline Kim. On the back cover, a black and white photo of a woman in a business suit smiled like she was saying hello. Ivy smiled back. Then, turning to hide her hand from her mom, she waved at the photo, returning Caroline's smile.

Then she felt silly.

It was the title of the book that had first interested Ivy. Then she researched the author. Dr. Kim, founder of the electronics and robotics company Sapai Industries, was everything Ivy wanted to be: smart, accomplished, successful. Ivy knew she, too, could get there one day. She had the fire in her belly, the drive to win. She just needed a plan. A success plan of her own. She immediately flipped the book open and started reading.

All too soon, they pulled into their garage. The giant old Victorian in the Western Addition neighborhood of San Francisco was divided into two condos. They'd lived in the large two bedroom top flat all Ivy's life, sharing the garage underneath with their neighbor.

Ivy dog-eared her page with a sigh and raced up the front steps, pausing only long enough to key in their door code.

"They should be here in about half an hour!" her mom's voice called from below.

Stairs disappeared under Ivy's feet two at a time. She

dropped the smelly gym bag at the top and brought the book to her room.

Math homework covered her bed, unfinished and accusing.

Ivy threw tonight's dress over it.

Sapphire satin with a V neck, the knee-length dress wrapped around, tying at her hip. Ivy assumed it was beautiful, judging from the little noises her friends and mom had made when she tried it on. But she liked it because it was comfortable and had pockets. It had probably been designed for someone a lot older, but it fit her well. Ivy was the oldest and tallest student in Lovelace's entire sixth grade. She would turn thirteen in June and had always been tall for her age. She was used to wearing clothes made for grown-ups.

A blue satin purse hung on the wall over her nightstand with three fabric flowers on the front. A paper program with the word 'Bespoke' written in swirly letters was push-pinned to the wall nearby. The purse's strap was a long, multicolored chain of finger-knitted yarn.

With a smile, she took it down and pushed aside a bit of fabric from between the pieces of the magnetic snap. The snap clicked closed.

The fabric flowers lit up.

She had invented the purse with Amber Rosenberg, one of her friends in the Renegade Girls Tinkering Club. She provided the electronic know-how, and Amber sewed the circuit with conductive thread. The purse had been the centerpiece of Amber's fashion collection, and Ivy wore it on the red carpet in Amber's youth internship competition.

Being a model had been more fun than Ivy thought it would be, and she was proud to have helped Amber understand the circuit they'd created to light up the flowers. Everyone should know a little bit about electricity since it was such an essential part of modern life.

Electricity was a primal force, a force of nature. A force people harnessed to get things done. Whether it was lighting up some flowers on a purse or powering a giant skyscraper, the concept was the same. Electricity always followed its own rules. Whether a circuit was simple like her flower purse or a complicated group of tons of circuits in a sophisticated piece of electronics, they all harnessed the same primal energy using the same basic concepts. With enough work Ivy could become more sophisticated, too. She just needed to harness her energy properly.

Or at least be at her friend's party on time.

Ivy turned off the purse's glowing flowers by slipping the fabric back between the metal snaps, breaking the flow of electricity in the circuit so the batteries wouldn't get used up. She set it on top of her new book.

Her math homework peeked out from under the dress, taunting her. When would she find time to help Benjamin with some giant school project? She couldn't even finish her homework. She didn't even have time to take a shower.

Reaching for the dress, Ivy caught a whiff of her own armpits.

Scratch that. Shower.

Now.

The icy water pelting over her was just starting to get warm as she stepped out and reached for a towel. She sighed as she turned it off. It was already 5:16.

Her other friends in the tinkering club, Kaminia Doyle and Wren Sterling, would pick her up at 5:30. And Kammie's mom was never late.

The satin dress slid over her head, smooth and cool. She pulled a brush through her still damp black hair with quick strokes, resisting the urge to pull it into its usual ponytail. But she did pop a hair band around her wrist like a bracelet, just in case. There was supposed to be dancing.

She stuffed *Success Plan* into her purse and turned to leave.

Then her gaze fell on the math homework waiting on her bed. When could she get to it? They were sleeping over at Kammie's after the party, then going straight to Wren's house for their club meeting. After that was this week's basketball game. It had to be done by Monday, and it was part of her grade for the class.

She stuffed the homework and a pencil inside her purse next to the book. Maybe she'd find an opportunity to work on it, and Ivy always liked to be prepared. Then she raced down the stairs just as Kammie's SUV pulled into her driveway.

2
PARTY DOWN

The northwestern tip of San Francisco, where the Pacific Ocean turned into the San Francisco Bay under the famous Golden Gate Bridge, had been a giant military base since the late 1700's. Back then, California belonged to Spain. But the Ohlone/Costanoan people, the original inhabitants of the area, had lived there for thousands of years before the arrival of Europeans. The Spanish had called their military base the *Presidio*, and the name stuck even after America took over. In 1994, the Presidio stopped being a military base and became a huge national park.

Kammie's SUV wove through its ribbon-like streets, towering trees, and old converted barracks, on the way to join Amber at the party.

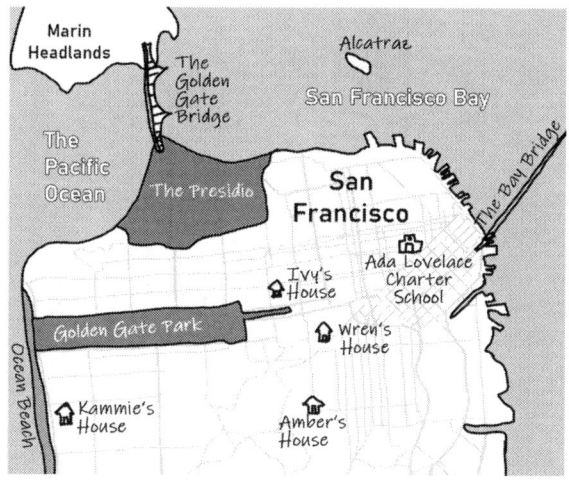

Ivy, Wren, and Kammie caught glimpses of the Golden Gate Bridge stretching majestically between San Francisco and the Marin Headlands. The red bridge glowed as the setting sun threw pinks, yellows, and purples across the few clouds in an almost clear sky. Out in the middle of the bay, Alcatraz Island's famous old prison peeked through the trees now and then. But the girls didn't even notice these sights that tourists traveled thousands of miles to see.

Instead, they talked about the party.

Amber's older brother Aiden had just turned thirteen and all the Renegades were invited to his Bar Mitzvah, probably to keep Amber out of his hair. Kammie's parents were coming too, to bring all four girls to Kammie's house afterwards for a sleepover. Plus, Ivy suspected Kammie's mom wouldn't have let her only child attend such a late party without her supervision.

Ivy had never been to a Bar Mitzvah before, but knew

it was a big deal. Aiden had been going to classes for years learning written Hebrew so he could read the Torah. He'd been doing his community service, and all the other things a Jewish child did when they transitioned to adulthood. Ivy respected the work he'd put in, and now it was paying off. His big moment. And they got to be a part of it.

"Amber's wearing one of the dresses she designed and sewed herself tonight," Wren told them. "That turquoise one with the wide straps and handkerchief hem. Her mom wasn't happy. She wanted her to buy something new, but you know Amber lately. She's all 'no way, that's bad for the environment!' I bet her mom got tired of fighting. Can you imagine being stuck in a house with Amber fighting about environmental stuff? It would be like trying to wash a cat."

Kammie giggled, then immediately covered her smile.

As usual, Kammie was guarding herself. Resisting her own internal energy. Sometimes, the electricity coursing through a circuit could overwhelm it. Small components called resistors kept the circuit from burning out or even exploding by limiting the flow of power. They were like blocking lanes on a busy highway, making all the traffic use a single lane. Kammie protected herself the same way. Only, her resistance was too strong. Ivy knew Kammie could really shine if she just let the current flow a little more. She wanted to help fix her resistors, all the other Renegades did too.

"Stop that," Wren pulled Kammie's hand away. "I like your teeth."

Kammie laughed even harder and blushed. But she didn't cover her mouth this time.

Wren, on the other hand, wasn't like a circuit, or even a battery. She was a force of nature, as unpredictable and powerful as lightning — or as annoying as static electricity. Wild and uncontrolled. Natural power so bright she could blind you, and you never knew where or when she would strike. Wren had so much potential. She just needed to focus, to try harder. Get organized. Ivy was always looking for ways to help fix her faulty connections, to help her be all she was capable of becoming.

The SUV pulled up to a beautiful white building. The sign out front said "The Golden Gate Club". A square, U-shaped building with a red Spanish tile roof surrounded a wide courtyard. Straight ahead, the back part of the building rose to a second floor. Everything glowed in the sunset.

They all piled out of the car and Ivy tugged her hoodie closer. The February day had been warm enough when the sun was out, but now a chill rode a light breeze in from the bay.

Without warning, Kammie's mom zipped up Ivy's hoodie. Then she snuggled her daughter into a down jacket, and reached to adjust Wren's coat. Wren grimaced at the reaching hands.

"No. Thanks. I'm okay," Wren pulled away and pointed to the front doors. "Look, it's there."

A big sign at the front doors read: WELCOME TO ADEN'S ROCK AND ROLL BAR MITZVAH, JOIN

US IN THE VENTANA ROOM. Next to the sign, Amber's mom was busy scolding a young man who held a tray of tiny hot dogs. The young waiter looked scared, eyes darting around nervously.

Someone cried out.

Amber was running towards them, arms outstretched, with one long squeal of greeting. Her asymmetrical skirt flared out as she barreled towards them, rhinestones glittering in her short auburn pixie hair.

"Honey, please," her mom snipped at her as she barreled past. "Inside voices."

Amber ignored her as the waiter grabbed the opportunity to escape into the building, quick as a slippery eel.

Amber's name was the first thing Ivy had noticed when she met her. The word 'electric' came from the Greek word for amber, the gemstone, because you can get a little electric charge if you rub amber with wool. Why anyone would rub amber with wool long enough to figure out this fact, Ivy had no idea, but it was true. And just like her namesake, Amber had an innate energy inside her that came out with a little polish. Amber had recently become what she called an "eco-warrior." Standing up for the environment. So now Ivy couldn't help but think of her as solar energy personified. Charging her own battery from the sun itself. Solar panels weren't very efficient technology, not yet, so Ivy helped Amber fix her efficiency at every opportunity.

"I'm so happy you're here!" Amber gushed. "Whoa, Kammie, are you wearing a *SARI*?"

Ivy blinked. She hadn't noticed anyone else's outfits.

Sure enough, Kammie wore a long burgundy silk skirt and a matching short sleeved shirt, decorated with ornate patterns in gold thread and studded with sparkling jewels. A long scarf draped over her shoulder and wrapped around her body, trapped under the puff of her down jacket. Ivy blinked again. How had she not noticed?

Kammie blushed and looked down at her golden flats.

"Wait," Wren narrowed her eyes at Kammie's mom. "Didn't you say you had to wait until you were sixteen to wear one of those?"

"Only in my family. Everyone's parents set their own rules," Kammie reminded her. Then she spun around with a glowing smile. "Mom gave me special permission tonight. Isn't it lovely?"

It was. The burgundy silk brought out Kammie's chestnut brown eyes and deep brown skin, and the gold highlighted her long black hair. Ivy suddenly realized how dressed up everyone else was, too. Other guests walked by in suits and long dresses. Even Wren had traded in her customary too-small stained jeans for a purple beaded dress, gray furry coat, and a large purse slathered with rhinestones. And for some reason, Wren also wore a purple bowtie.

Kammie's mom wore a deep navy sari with silver trim. Her dad had gone to park the car, but Ivy thought she remembered him wearing a matching navy tie.

Just then, two boys in well-tailored suits rushed by, laughing. The smaller one chased the older one.

"Boys!" yelled Amber's mom. The boys stopped in their tracks. "Walk please."

One gangly boy, Amber's younger brother Blaise, looked a lot like a puppy, with huge hands and feet, and short, fluffy red hair. He pointed to the sign.

"Look Aiden!" Blaise erupted in laughter again. "They spelled your name wrong! It's your own party and they spelled your name wrong!"

Amber's older brother lunged at Blaise. "Shut up!"

Blaise took off with Aiden close behind, yelling threats.

"Real mature," Amber yelled after Aiden. "I thought you were an adult now, butthead."

Amber's mom looked at the sign and gasped.

"I KNEW they'd do this!" she groaned. "I mean honestly, 'Aden'? I went over it with them four times for heaven's sake."

"They typo'ed the guest of honor?" Wren asked, reading the sign again. "I hadn't even noticed."

"What? Oh, hi sweetheart," Amber's mom suddenly noticed the group in front of her. She thanked them for coming in a well-practiced way and turned back to the sign. "It's not really a typo, it's the more common Jewish way to spell Aiden."

"But," Wren wrinkled her forehead, "then why is his name spelled with an I?"

Amber's mom laughed. "Ironically, we decided to name him Aiden-with-an-I instead of Aden-without-an-I so people would spell it correctly! Excuse me, I have to go find someone to yell at."

She looked around for the waiter she'd been talking with earlier. Growling through gritted teeth, she somehow stomped away in her high heeled shoes. Ivy had to admire her athletic prowess. She'd probably break her neck.

Waiters with trays skittered out of Amber's mom's way as she bellowed for someone named Emile.

"I hadn't noticed the spelling either," Kammie's mom told the girls.

Amber scowled as her mother terrorized another waiter. She twirled a finger near her head and rolled her eyes.

"Mom's been like this all weekend. Bossing everyone around. I swear she's going to explode by the end of the night," Amber grabbed Wren and Kammie by the hands, pulling them across the hall. "Come on, we're gonna have so much fun!"

Music, lights, and laughter spilled from the open door.

Ivy followed them into the room. And froze in her tracks.

3

AIDEN'S WORLD TOUR

The vast room twinkled.
A disco ball hung from the high rafters scattering bubbles of light over dozens of finely set round tables. More tables, long and rectangular, flanked the dance floor. Windows stretched from the floor to the lofted ceiling. Through them, the sun painted the towering trees outside with the last golden light of the evening's final show.

To their left, Aiden and some friends looked through the song list at a karaoke machine. More friends clustered on small couches around the machine's giant screen as Aiden and his crew began their song.

Grown-ups wandered among the elegant tables, looking for their names on little cards and swarming a bar set against the windows. A bartender poured glass after glass as the crowd of adults multiplied.

On a stage above the dance floor, fourteen tall glass vases filled with red liquid surrounded giant, lit-up wooden letters that spelled out AIDEN. A single unlit candle floated in each vase.

"Those are for the candle lighting ceremony," Amber explained. "People who've been important in Aiden's life go up in thirteen different groups and say something, then light a candle. I have to go up there and publicly say nice things about my brother."

"There are fourteen candles," Wren counted.

"The last one's for luck. Besides apparently fourteen candles look better behind his stupid name," Amber rolled her eyes.

"At least they spelled it right this time," Ivy pointed out.

"The long tables are for the kids. Let's grab a good spot." Amber led the way to some prime corner-table real estate.

"This sure is fancy," Wren sighed.

Amber shrugged. "It better be, for all the stress it's causing mom. This is just a small taste of the weekend too. Family flew in all week long doing the tourist thing. We had Shabbat on Friday, brunch and services this morning, and now this party. There's going to be a breakfast thing tomorrow morning too, to say goodbye to everybody. I'm so glad I'll be with you guys at Kammie's house. I need a break!"

"Oh Amber! What a special night." Kammie spun

around. Her silk scarf, freed from the puffy down jacket, billowed around her. "Your brother must be so excited."

Ivy sat with her back to the dance floor and pulled *Success Plan* out of her purse. "Are Bar Mitzvahs always so...big?"

"Nah," Amber shook her head. "My cousin Liam's was in a bowling alley. I loved it. Totally low key. Something like twelve kids, and Aunt Sarah didn't run around bossing people and going crazy. My mom just likes to make a big deal out of things."

"What's yours going to be like?" Wren grabbed a tiny hot dog off a passing tray and shoved it in her mouth. "Tell me you're gonna have food like this."

"I said I wanted an environmental theme, but Mom laughed. I'll convince her, eventually. I mean it's MY Bat Mitzvah. But I need to really start preparing though. I'm already busy enough with working at Bygone plus all the homework we have this year."

"I've been pretty busy too," Kammie began, barely audible over the music.

"Oh hey, that reminds me," Ivy looked up from her book. "I ran into Benjamin earlier."

Amber froze.

"Benjamin Spencer?" She squeaked.

"Yeah, I sort of promised we'd help him with Career Week. I'm sorry guys, I know I shouldn't have spoken for everyone, but he was pretty persistent. He wants to talk to us on Monday."

Wren punched Amber in the shoulder. "I guess you'll

have to make time now. Don't want to miss an opportunity to hang out with Beeeenjamin."

"We should at least see what he wants," Amber glared, the color rising in her cheeks. "It's only polite. I mean he did help us when we had our spy business."

"Speaking of stuff," Kammie began again. "We have a lot going on at my house—"

Just then, Blaise ran up. "Amber! I'm getting a tattoo! Should I get a tiger or a snake?"

"There are TATTOOS?!" Wren dropped her purse on the table with a clatter. "Where? WHERE?!"

Blaise pointed.

"I'll be right back, guys!" Wren tugged on Blaise's arm. "Let's go, little man."

Ivy tried to find her place in *Success Plan* again. It was hard to read with everyone buzzing around but she couldn't stop. The book was fascinating. Aiden arrived with a tray full of glasses of a red, sparkling drink. Ice cubes shaped like guitars bobbed around in each glass, bumping into tall, skinny, paper straws.

"Have a drink," he set down the tray and took one himself. "Don't worry, it's non-alcoholic."

"Mom has you delivering drinks at your own party?" Amber picked one up and sucked on the straw. "She's losing her mind."

Aiden handed a glass to Ivy, who closed the book with a frown. Kammie accepted a glass, too.

"I'm just helping out. Being a mensch," Aiden sipped

his drink. "You should really lay off Mother, Amber. She's working really hard."

"Exactly," Amber fumed. "Why is she working so hard? The party's just fine. It doesn't have to be perfect. She's being so bossy."

"You haven't called Emile bossy," Aiden pointed out. "And he's the one who's been barking orders all weekend."

"That's his JOB," Amber bristled. "He's the event planner. It's not Mom's job to tell everyone what to do."

Aiden looked around his party. The sun had fully set. Lights shimmered outside the giant window and inside the giant room. Adults continued to crowd around the bar while kids swarmed the karaoke station and sat at tables sipping red drinks. Blaise chased a few of the younger ones around the empty dance floor.

"You see Great-Aunt Bernice over there?" Aiden pointed to a gray-haired woman talking with their dad. "How many more trips to San Francisco do you think she's gonna make?"

Amber shrugged.

"All these people," Aiden continued. "They came here for me. But if they don't have fun, do you know who's going to get judged? Not me. Mom. I'm not the one dealing with Emile, or the DJ, or the photographer. I'm not the one who squeezed in planning this event for a year alongside my regular job. And I'm not the one paying for it."

"So she's freaking out because she doesn't want people to judge her?" Amber asked. "I thought we weren't supposed to care about what other people think."

"Amber, Amber, Amber," Aiden patted her on the head. She glared at him. "Of course she wants people to like the party. But it's more than that. All these people, Great-Aunt Bernice, Aunt Molly and Uncle Tim, Aunt Sarah's whole family. There are almost two hundred people here. And you know what? Mom loves every single one of them. Even you, stinkbutt. You'll understand someday, when you're older. This is a big deal to her, and she wants it to be special for everyone. And you just call her bossy. It's not fair."

Amber grew quiet, watching their mom chat with Aunt Molly. "When did you get so mature?"

"I'm an adult now," Aiden stuck his tongue out at Amber. Then he grabbed the tray and disappeared into the crowd.

Ivy shook her head and opened her book again, but it had gotten too dark to read. Ivy's sigh was lost in the music as she stuffed the book in her glowing purse. Maybe there was just enough light to finish her math homework. If she could get it out of the way now, she'd be able to enjoy the party. She dug inside her purse for it but a loud groan and stomping feet made her look up.

"That henna tattoo lady won't paint a cat tattoo on my face," Wren waved her arms around angrily. Kammie took a step back, but Amber giggled as Wren continued. "It's FAKE. It's a fake tattoo, and I should be able to get it wherever I want."

"I think it's pretty," Kammie gently touched Wren's bicep, where the cat tattoo had ended up.

"I guess if it had ended up on my face I would have to carry around a mirror to look at it." Wren craned her neck to look at the cat. "Okay, I guess I'll forgive her. But oh my gosh, guys, have you seen the party favors?"

Wren grabbed Ivy's purse and plopped it on her plate. Ivy looked at the homework sticking halfway out. It was hard to enjoy the party with the unfinished work hanging over her head. But Wren yanked Ivy out of her chair and grabbed Amber's arm, bumping Kammie with her butt, trying to drag the whole group with her. Ivy tried to put the homework out of her mind but it sat there like a persistent beep in the background of her thoughts calling *finish me, finish me first, then you can relax*. She shook her head and followed Wren.

Groups of kids, and a few adults, swarmed the back corner of the room. Actual instruments were set up on a fake stage, surrounded by lights and cameras. It was the fanciest photo booth Ivy had ever seen. A group of kids rushed onto the stage, grabbing guitars, microphones, and fighting over the drum set. One of them stood behind a standing electric keyboard and began mashing on the keys.

They posed, lights flashed, and then made room for another group.

"What's your band name, honey?" a tired looking man behind the camera asked Amber when it was their turn.

"The Renegades!" shouted Wren. The man nodded with approval and motioned them onto the stage.

Wren rushed to the drum kit and started wailing on the drums while Amber took up the lead singer position and Kammie hid behind the keyboard. Ivy watched them pose and giggle, but her mind kept drifting back to her homework. She grabbed a guitar and, on a whim, strummed it. A buzzy chord rewarded her.

It was kind of fun, actually. She pushed her fingers against the fretboard and strummed a few more times, a smile poking through her serious expression. She strummed harder and, just for a moment, forgot about the math calling to her from the table. Maybe she could find some time to take guitar lessons.

"POSE, Renegades!" the man yelled.

Ivy looked up at the camera in shock. Lights flashed. They did three more poses, and picked their favorite. Then the photo, with the band name superimposed on top, was printed out four times onto special paper. A woman grabbed a shirt that said "Aiden's World Tour" with a bunch of dates on the back, and used a hot press to apply the photo to the front. Soon they each had their own band shirt. It was the most amazing party favor Ivy had ever seen.

Maybe, just for a while, she could forget about her homework, her book, and enjoy the party...

DINNER WAS DELICIOUS, and the candle lighting ceremony was interesting, even if it did drag on a little long. The dance floor opened and the DJ spun some great music. Everyone rushed out to the dance floor.

Except Ivy.

She'd made it through most of the party, but the persistent mental tug of unfinished tasks eventually wore her down. Now, she sat at the table, *Success Plan* next to her, trying to focus on her math homework and ignore the thumping bass from the dance floor.

Wren stumbled to the table to grab some water, her hair a wild mess around her flushed and sweaty face. As soon as she saw Ivy, she slammed the glass down, sploshing water onto the tablecloth.

"You can't do HOMEWORK at a PARTY, Ivy!" Wren grabbed the pencil out of her hand. "Geeze! That's terrible!"

"Hey," Ivy growled, reaching for the pencil. "Give that back NOW young lady!"

"Quit being so bossy and join the fun," Wren held the pencil over her head.

Ivy, much taller, plucked the pencil out of her grip. "Just let me finish number 16."

Wren sat across from her and crossed her arm, leveling Ivy with a serious stare. "I am not moving until you come dance."

Ivy ignored her.

Wren reached over and grabbed two pieces of paper from Ivy's stack. She folded one into a triangle and tore off the extra paper edge, unfolding it again to reveal a square. Then she did the same with the other piece.

Wren picked up one triangle and made fold after fold with fast, practiced creases as Ivy tried to ignore her. Soon,

Wren had two origami shapes. She set one shape in front of Ivy, and balanced the other on top. Ivy looked up. She couldn't help it.

Before her sat a little paper cat. It stared at her, the paper head balanced on a pointy neck.

"You've memorized how to fold that origami?" Ivy asked.

"It's a cat, Ivy." Wren replied. She wiggled the cat's paper head as if it, too, were dancing to the music.

Ivy looked at everyone else dancing. Singing. Laughing.

"Cat is dancing, Ivy. Be like cat. Cat wants you to dance, too," Wren informed her. "'Come dance with Wren,' says cat."

"Cut it out, Wren, this is important."

"Don't disappoint cat, Ivy. That never ends well. You need to have some fun." Wren lifted the cat in front of her face and spoke in a high-pitched voice as if the cat spoke. "This is a party. You DESERVE to have some fun. Do it another time."

Ivy looked down at her math. "There is no other time."

"Cat isn't listening to you, Ivy, are you cat?" Wren shook the cat's paper head no. "See? Cat is wise. Listen to cat."

Ivy looked at the dance floor. Amber bounced to the beat and screamed out lyrics with her eyes closed. Kammie swayed happily next to her. She noticed Ivy watching them and waved, motioning for her to join them. Ivy glanced at her homework again.

She set down her pencil.

"You're right," she nodded.

Her words were drowned out by the throb of music as Wren grabbed her hands and dragged her onto the dance floor.

ORIGAMI

MATERIALS
- 2 sheets of origami paper
  -OR-
- 2 squares of any kind of paper

OPTIONAL
- Scissors
- Pen, marker, or googly eyes

KEY
- ▓ - outside of pap[er]
- ☐ - inside of pape[r]
- - - - - fold line
- ↻ - flip over
- ➤ - fold direction

The Body

① Fold one square in half diagonally then unfold. Fold in the corners to line up with the center fold

② Fo[ld] alo[ng] th[e] cent[er] creas[e] foldi[ng] the fla[p] towar[d] the insi[de]

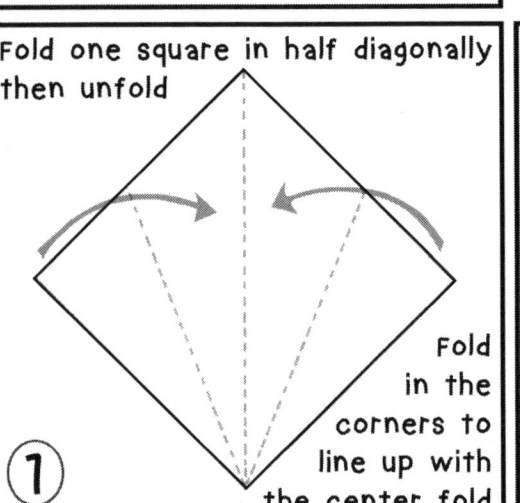

③ Fold the bottom point up to overlap the top edge a little bit

④ Fold that point down at an angle to stick up past the folded edge

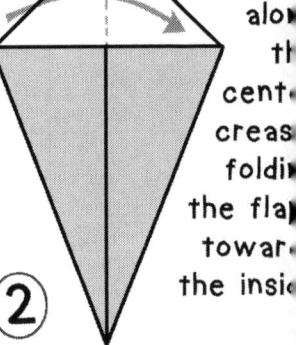

⑤ Fold th[e] point so stic[k] ov[er] the fold[ed] paper. Tha[t's the] kitty's t[ail]

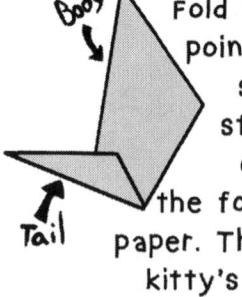

KITTY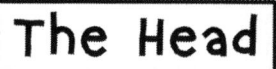

The Head

1) Fold and unfold the other square both ways, then fold the top point down to the middle

2) Fold top half down, and fold a bit of the bottom corner back behind the square

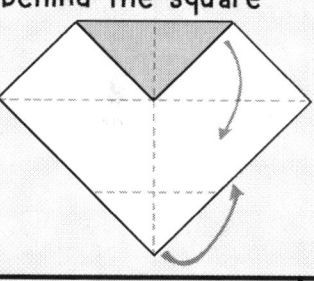

Fold each corner down so the folded edge aligns with your middle fold line

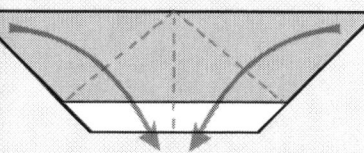

5) Fold down the top and flip it over

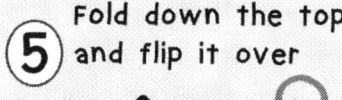

Now fold them again, halfway up so the points stick up over the head. These are kitty's ears

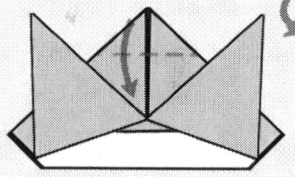

6) Fold over the tip to make a little nose, draw some eyes. Place the head on the body. Kitty!

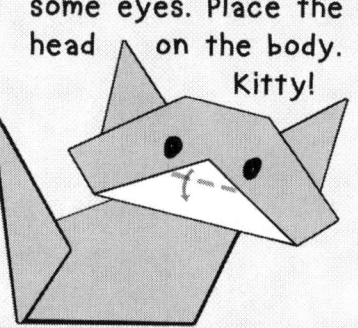

4

BENJAMIN'S IDEA

"Ivy, will you put that stupid book down?" Wren grabbed *Success Plan* and turned it upside down, squinting at the pages. "How can you read this so much? There's not even any story in there!"

"Wren!" Kammie gasped. "Give that back! What are you doing?"

"Stooory? Are you in there?" Wren called, shaking the book as if little characters might fall from the pages and dance for her. "There isn't even a single dragon or cat at all."

"Give it to me now." Ivy's voice tinged with annoyance, and even a bit of desperation. "Lunch is the only time I have to read it!"

It was Monday. The girls waited for Benjamin to come find them at their usual green picnic table while kids bubbled around them on Lovelace's playground. Sunshine beat down on the kids swarming the squishy-floored climbing structure, the tables, and the basketball area. Lovelace went from kindergarten all the way up to eighth grade. The playground was always packed, and Monday's lunch period was no exception.

Even so, the Renegades almost always ate outside. Wren hated the cafeteria. She said it was too loud, too bright, and smelled like other kid's lunches. But they all liked the fresh air. And ever since they'd had their own spy gadget business, they'd had an unspoken claim to this particular picnic table.

They had no idea where Benjamin usually ate, but Ivy assumed he spent his lunch period organizing something or meeting with his student council.

When Ivy thought about Benjamin, a computer's motherboard sprang to mind. A motherboard was the main part of a computer. And just like a motherboard, Benjamin brought together important components, helped them all work with each other, managed the input (information that came into the system) and output (information that came out of it), and acted as a Central Processing Unit (CPU). In other words, he processed information by deciding what information went where, at what time, and how it got to its destination. Just like the way a Motherboard supports and links together memory, graphics, and specialty components.

Benjamin was a leader. That's what Ivy respected the most about him. Her motherboard comparison wasn't a perfect analogy, but it made sense to her. In fact, *Success Plan* had mentioned something about a leader being like a motherboard in one of the first chapters. Ivy went to look it up, and realized Wren still had her book. She was rubbing it on her head, mumbling something about transferring ideas.

"Give. Now." Ivy stood and yanked the book from her friend's head. "I'd read a biography about Caroline Kim any day, but *Success Plan* is about how to plan for your future success. Step by step..."

"Sounds BOOOOORING," Wren's yawn was loud enough to be heard over the playground noise. "A future without a dragon does not sound very successful to me."

"You're hilarious," Ivy opened the book. "Look, Dr. Kim is a genius. She's a lot like me, actually. Second generation Korean-American with a single mother. She even played varsity soccer."

"Oh, so you're a genius now?" Wren punched her in the shoulder with a smile.

"Smarter than you," Ivy punched her back. "Seriously, this book has all kinds of hints and tips on how to plan out your whole career. Don't you guys want to be successful? It's full of interesting stories about her life, things she's had to deal with. Inspiration. You don't know what you're missing."

Amber lay on top of the table, her head dangling upside down over the edge. Her lunchbox, filled with leftover hors d'œuvres from the party, sat beside her. She'd only eaten a few bites. "Do you think he's coming?"

"Who?" Wren shoved more bagel in her mouth.

"Who?!?" Amber sat up and stared at her. "Are you kidding me?"

"Oh." She pointed to a figure approaching through the crowd. "You mean that guy?"

Benjamin walked right through a group of kids shooting hoops. Someone called to him and threw him their ball. He caught it, dribbled once, and took a shot at the basket. Ivy perked up, analyzing his form. Shooting a basketball was as much about the angles of the elbows and wrists as it was about the power behind the shot. But she could tell immediately by the ball's trajectory that it wasn't going in.

Sure enough, the ball bounced off the backboard. Benjamin shrugged as one of the kids ran to retrieve the wayward ball. They waved and resumed their game. Ivy shook her head. He handled defeat so easily. She wished she could be so level-headed.

"Hey, great to see you all." Benjamin leaned against the green wooden picnic table and got right to business. "Here's my idea. Tell me what you think. I've had a lot going on, but this takes top priority now. I want the upcoming Career Week to be the best it can be and I need all the help I can get."

"What do you have going on?" Wren tore off another hunk of bagel.

"Getting ready to head to Babbage High next year," Benjamin's face grew serious. "I really want this Career Week to be something special, make my mark, you know.

Leave my legacy. I don't have any great ideas yet, but I don't want Lovelace to forget me."

His voice faded.

"Who could ever forget you?" Amber reassured him quickly. "That's just crazy."

"Thanks," he shook his head and refocused on them. "So, anyway, I'd really like your help. Principal Sophie is onboard to go all out. Have the teachers wrap whatever activities we come up with for Career Week into classes. Do assemblies. Get the whole school involved."

"What do you need from us, then?" Ivy asked.

"And also? Even though I'd love to help any way I can, I don't have a lot of time," Amber winced. "Sorry. I have my internship and school. Plus I need to get serious about preparing for my Bat Mitzvah. It's getting pretty intense."

"I'm going to be busy too," Kammie began in her quiet voice. "Pretty soon."

"Well, I've got nothing going on," Wren shrugged.

"I won't ask for much," Benjamin replied. "Just a little of your creative spark. You Renegades always come up with such clever ideas. How do you think them up?"

"Oh, we brainstorm," Wren wiped cream cheese off her cheek. "We all get together in the Greenhouse, that's our workshop in my backyard. We call it that because it used to be a greenhouse. I guess that's kind of obvious. But anyway, we all get around Trixie's old art easel. Trixie is my little sister. You remember, the one who made the spy lollipop? We have a roll of paper we pull over the art easel and Kammie, who has really good handwriting, she writes down all our ideas as we think them up. There's more to it than that. First..."

"You can help us brainstorm, then?" Benjamin set his hand on Wren's arm to apologize as he interrupted her. "That would definitely be helpful."

"Maybe," Ivy hesitated. "We've never really brainstormed with anyone outside our club. Except when it's a class project."

"Well, if it's just brainstorming," Wren said, "I can vomit out all kinds of ideas. Some of them are actually good, too."

Ivy nodded. "We'll do what we can."

"Great," Benjamin glanced at the clock on his cell phone. "I have to run, I've got a thing. Why don't you join me after school today? Gail secured some library space so we could talk through some ideas. See you there!"

He meant Gail Mendez. She ran the school newspaper, the *Lovelace Gazette,* and was their other eighth grade friend. Ivy immediately understood why it would be important to get Gail involved. Kids loved the newspaper, whether online or the physical copies she brought to the lunch room every Thursday. Everyone read the paper. If Benjamin wanted to get information out to the school, going through his friend Gail was the easiest route.

He disappeared into the crowd of kids as quickly as he'd appeared, leaving them staring after him. Wondering what they'd just agreed to.

"Sooo," Kammie turned to the others. "I guess we're helping?"

"Tonight seems pretty short notice but I don't have basketball practice," Ivy shrugged. "I just have to be home in time to make dinner. It's my night tonight."

"It's just a little brainstorm," Kammie added. "It would be nice to see Gail again."

"It'll be just like old times!" Amber agreed. "When we all worked together to uncover the election thief back at the beginning of the year. Just the six of us against the world. I'm sure I can convince my mom to let me go. It'll be fun! Ivy, can I borrow your phone?"

It was true, Ivy thought. Being accused of stealing the student election results had been awful, but working with Gail and Benjamin to try and find the real culprit had been fun. Maybe a little time spent brainstorming with them would be fun, too.

"Yeah," Wren nudged Amber. "What could possibly go wrong."

"There's a whole chapter on brainstorming in here," Ivy waved *Success Plan* at them. "I'll skim it for ideas."

"Why?" Wren finished her bagel and packed up her lunchbox. "We brainstorm all the time. It can't be that different with Gail and Benjamin."

"It's always good to be prepared," Kammie pointed out. "I think it's a great idea to read up on ideas."

"So are we doing this?" Ivy paused, her fingers poised over the keypad of her cell phone. As the others nodded, she hit send on the text to her mom, then handed the phone to Amber. Her cell phone was the only one they had. Everyone had to share it.

Ivy found the chapter on brainstorming and started reading again as the girls took turns calling their parents.

She'd only read two pages when the lunch monitor blew his whistle. Ivy sighed. All the kids started streaming back into the school. Ivy stuffed her thermos, chopsticks, and the rest of her containers back into her lunch bag and stood up.

Just a brainstorming session. It was the least she could do for Benjamin, for the school. And Amber was right. It was just a few friends getting together, thinking up ideas.

Really. What could go wrong?

They met at Wren's locker after school to walk to the library together.

"This is going to be so fun!" Amber gushed. "Just the six of us, catching up and coming up with great ideas. I can't wait, I'm so glad Benjamin asked us to join him and Gail."

Ivy nodded. "I have to admit, I'm looking forward to it. I know it's a little silly, but it feels nice to be singled out. It shows Benjamin really sees our potential."

"I'm starting to feel comfortable around the two of them," Kammie agreed. "Like I'll really be able to be helpful."

Benjamin was just closing his locker when the girls walked up. He waved. The only things in his hands were a notebook and a pen. Ivy looked down at *Success Plan* and tucked it under the notebook she had brought for taking notes.

"I'm so glad you could join us!" Benjamin strode

towards the library. "Everyone will be so happy to see you."

"Everyone?" Amber paused, then jogged to catch up. "Umm. Who else is going to be there?"

Benjamin opened the library door and motioned them inside. The room was packed. There must have been twenty or thirty people. Ivy recognized the whole student council, half the swim team, and some of the newspaper staff. Gail Mendez waved at them as they entered. She was just setting up an easel with paper rolled over it, not unlike the one the Renegades used in the Greenhouse.

"There they are," Gail told the crowd. "Our experts! Everybody give a big warm welcome to the Renegade Girls Tinkering Club!"

Noise filled the room. There was some smattering of applause, a little mumbling, and some chatter. But every head in the room turned to look at them.

Wren gulped audibly.

"Nope," Kammie mumbled. She turned around and walked right back out.

5

TAKING CHARGE

Wren followed Kammie out the door.

Amber looked at Benjamin and everyone gathered around. She glanced at the door, her eyebrows knotting together. She turned back to Benjamin without a word, looking like she was in pain. She bit her lip, shrugged, and turned her helpless palms up to the crowd, turned, and ran after her friends.

Gail sighed.

Ivy glanced back at the hallway and turned towards the waiting crowd. "Hello! So happy to see you all. Umm. We forgot something. Something important. Will you please excuse us for just a little second? Thanks so much."

Ivy closed the door to the library behind her as she joined the others in the hall.

"What are you doing?" She erupted at Kammie, and immediately regretted it.

Kammie leaned against the wall, staring at nothing,

breathing heavily. She was quietly whispering "I'm sorry, I'm sorry, I'm sorry," over and over again.

Wren stood in front of her, demonstrating slow breaths. She reached out and took Kammie's hands.

"It's okay," she told Kammie. "It's just fine."

Ivy and Amber looked at each other.

"Look, Kammie," Ivy began. "I know it's not what we expected, but we can do this. We can roll with it. You're strong, Kam. Stronger than you give yourself credit for."

"I'm sorry," Kammie repeated, looking Wren in the eyes and breathing with her. "It just caught me by surprise. I... I don't think I can go back in there. Too many people. They were all looking at me."

Ivy glanced at the door. Through the window she could see Benjamin talking to the crowd. They laughed. He headed over to the door and opened it big enough to stick his head out.

"Everything okay?" he sounded worried.

"We're fine," Ivy replied.

"No," Wren said, not turning away from Kammie. "We're not. We didn't expect so many people. We thought it was just going to be you and Gail. Why did you lie?"

"Wren!" Amber gasped. "He didn't LIE. We misunderstood. Sorry Benjamin."

Benjamin rubbed the back of his neck. "Gosh, I'm sorry. I've been so busy, I guess I didn't realize... umm. But are you still going to help?"

Ivy motioned him back inside the door. "Give me a second. We'll be fine."

"Okay, I'll cover for you," Benjamin closed the library door.

Ivy turned back to the other Renegades. "Come on you guys. I know it's not what we were expecting, but we're here now. All we can do is roll with it. Besides, what a great opportunity to shine! Dr. Kim says it's important to grab an opportunity when you can, because they don't come by every day."

"But we don't know how to lead strangers in a brainstorm," Kammie whispered furtively. "We've never done anything like that. How do we even start?"

"Let's just give it a try," Ivy shrugged. "The *Success Plan* chapter on brainstorming covered a lot of group techniques. See how helpful Dr. Kim can be? Besides, she says success is all about confidence. Fake it till you make it."

"I'm in," Amber set a hand on Kammie's arm. "Why don't you just come out with us? You don't have to say anything, we've got you. Just come be part of the team."

"This is dumb," Wren griped.

"No," Kammie closed her eyes. "It's okay. I'm sorry, it just caught me by surprise. Now I'm embarrassed. But if you guys are ready, so am I."

"Thata girl!" Ivy clapped her shoulder. She turned to make sure Wren was okay too.

Wren nodded. "Let's do this."

Ivy opened the door and led the way back inside.

Benjamin nodded to them. He stood at the front of the crowd with a casual smile, as if nothing was wrong. All the chairs seemed to be taken. The Renegades looked around awkwardly, not sure where to sit. Benjamin smiled at them and motioned towards the wall next to him. They hesitantly stepped over and stood there, huddled together.

"I think you all know these girls," He spoke to the larger group, gesturing towards them. "The geniuses in the Renegade Girls Tinkering Club."

Wren snorted.

"We're not geniuses," Amber corrected quietly. "At least I'm not."

"Don't be so modest," Benjamin smiled indulgently. "Look at all you guys have accomplished in just your first year in Middle School. You've got great things in your future."

Amber blushed and turned away, mumbling, "We've been lucky, I guess."

"Anyway," Benjamin continued unperturbed, "These girls are experts at brainstorming, so I thought I'd bring them in to lead us in a brainstorm session to get this Career Week planning kicked off right! Let's give them a big hand."

Applause spattered throughout the crowd as Benjamin turned to them and clapped loudly. He held a marker out towards them. "Shall we get started?"

Ivy took a deep breath, stood up straight, and smiled at the crowd. She strode forward, taking the marker and, on a whim, shook Benjamin's hand. A flash lit up from somewhere in the crowd, from Gail's general direction.

The marker sat heavy in her hand. Kammie was usually the one who wrote everything down. All Ivy and the others usually had to do was shout out whatever came into their heads. She glanced down at the marker as the crowd watched them expectantly. Silently. More than a few kids in the audience had notebooks and pens or laptops out, ready to take notes.

It was time to make a decision for real. Was she going to show up or go home? Just like in a basketball or soccer game, you never had control over your circumstances. Sometimes a shot opened up that you never expected, one that wasn't in the plans. Grabbing the shot when it appeared could mean the difference between winning or losing the game. Ivy took another deep breath. What's the worst that could happen?

But how to start?

When the Renegades brainstormed, it was usually the first step towards a goal. At the beginning of the year, they'd discovered the Engineering Design Process. First they had to figure out the right question to ask, which could be more complicated than it seemed. Then they brainstormed to come up with all the ideas they could, even if those ideas weren't going to work. Sometimes crazy ideas helped people think of workable ones. Then they'd look over the ideas and pick what worked, and make a prototype to test and evaluate.

But they weren't engineering anything here. Would the same process apply? If they were just trying to think up ideas, the whole engineering design process was overkill. Caroline Kim said a brainstorm was where you established your foundation, and to do that you had to simplify. To bring an idea down to its most basic components. Which came back to the idea of the question. To get the right answer, you had to ask the right question.

"Okay," she began in a clear, strong voice that surprised her. "What's the problem?"

The other kids looked at each other. One girl, named Afsheen, tilted her head. She and the boy sitting next to her, Tyrone, had won the student elections at the start of the year. The elections the Renegades had been accused of stealing, back when their business selling spy gear catapulted them to brief but spectacular popularity. Their own invented spy gear that had proved their innocence and captured the real thief.

"What do you mean?" Afsheen asked. "There's no problem. We're trying to think up ideas."

"Exactly," Ivy smiled. "Asking the right question. That's how we start."

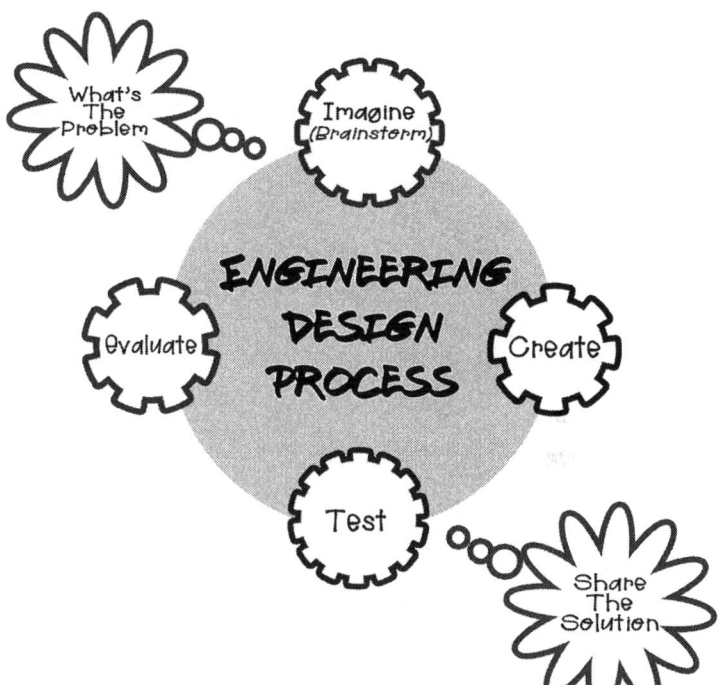

6

BRAINSTORM

"A brainstorm doesn't mean just sitting around chatting," Ivy explained. "And it's not a free-for-all. Every successful brainstorm follows a few rules."

She'd just read that in the brainstorming chapter. The Renegades never specifically set rules, but somehow still ended up following the same guidelines that Dr. Kim laid out in the chapter. Ivy pulled the cap off her marker and wrote as she talked. Her handwriting wasn't as quick or readable as Kammie's, but it was the best she could do under the circumstances.

1. Set a time limit.
2. Know your goal.
3. Write everything down.
4. Everyone participates.
5. Have a leader.
6. List every idea, no matter what. No judgments.

That last was important. Actually, they were all important. Ivy put the cap back on her marker and used it to tap on the words she'd just written as she went over the list.

"So, you can see that the rules are still pretty open ended. The trick to a successful brainstorm is to get the ideas flowing. You never know when an idea you thought was crazy will spark a different idea that turns out to be brilliant." Ivy looked around at the faces watching her, trying another trick from the book — to meet everyone's gaze for just a few seconds. It was a little awkward at first, but she tried to at least glance over the whole crowd. It would have to do.

"We have an hour," Benjamin offered. "So maybe 30 minutes doing actual brainstorming would be a good time limit."

Ivy wrote it down on the board.

"The next part is really important," Ivy tapped number two. "Know your goal. We should be really clear about what we're trying to solve here."

"We're trying to give Ben a big sendoff," Gail offered. "Oh, wait. I'm not here to participate. I'm just covering it for the paper, sorry."

"But that's not the goal," Wren squeaked. She cleared her throat a few times, then continued with a stronger voice. "Maybe that's A goal, but it's not THE goal, right?"

A few kids nodded. Some of the others clicked away at their keyboards. Ivy was pretty sure a few of them were checking social media.

"We're trying to think up ideas for Career Week," Afsheen declared. "Pretty straightforward."

"But what kind of ideas?" Wren pointed out. "Like, names of careers? Ideas to make money for scholarships or internships or something else? Ideas on how to get a job? Ideas for activities or posters?"

Afsheen squinched her eyebrows together in confusion. "That's a good point."

"I can answer that," Benjamin addressed everyone, "What we need right now are ideas for ways to introduce different career options, and what it might be like to work in those careers."

Everyone nodded. Ivy tried to write it down, but then forgot Benjamin's wording. She started to ask him to repeat it, but a quiet hand gently pulled the marker from her grip. She hadn't even noticed Kammie walk up.

"Are you okay?" she mouthed.

Kammie nodded, and quickly wrote down what Benjamin had said. She had a lot more experience.

Ivy sighed with relief and looked at the board again. Next one. *Everyone participates.* That could be a problem. Only a few of the people in the library seemed to be paying attention. To be fair, it was after school and everyone was tired. And there were a lot of kids here. Most of them probably only showed up to impress Benjamin. It was easy for the less motivated to lose themselves in the crowd. But Caroline Kim had emphasized how important it was to make sure every single person felt heard. To get everyone involved.

She looked out into the crowd, and her mind visualized everyone as a circuit. Just one circuit wasn't that useful. To do anything more than turn on a tiny light or buzz a buzzer, you needed lots of them, all working together.

But wait... if she thought of the group as a bunch of individual parts working together maybe she could figure out how to reach every one of them. Every person here needed input and output, energy to go in, and an idea to come back out.

If she wanted to run multiple electrical components from a single power source, she would either rig it in a series or parallel circuit.

A series circuit was like a string of Christmas lights. The power went in and out of each light, one after the other.

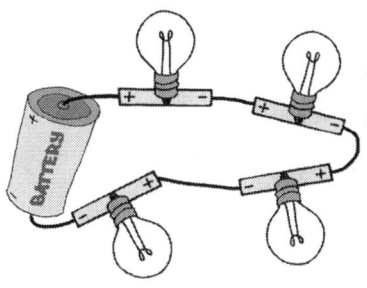

Ivy tried to count the number of people in the crowd. Giving every person a turn to say something round-robin style would take way too long.

But what if they worked in parallel?

In a parallel circuit, components branched off a single

line of energy. The power ran up one side, and down the other, while the components connected their positive lead to the positive energy flow, and their negative lead into the negative energy flow.

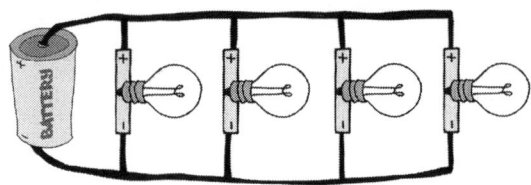

Because electricity moved so fast, the components all got their power at pretty much the same time, even though each component got less energy because they all had to share. It was like a bunch of swimmers swimming in different lanes next to each other, rather than taking turns in the same swim lane. It used up a lot more of the pool, and was harder to coordinate, but the swimmers didn't have to wait around. It wasn't only more efficient, working in parallel, whether with a circuit or a bunch of swimmers, also made things more stable. If something broke, like a component burned out or a dog jumped into one of the swim lanes and blocked it, the whole thing could keep going. The other components kept doing whatever they did or the swimmers could just use the other lanes.

Maybe the group could divide into smaller groups, each with its own leader, and work at the same time... in parallel. Then the groups could get back together at the end and share their ideas. It wasn't how the Renegades usually brainstormed, but this time wasn't like sitting around in their Greenhouse. Would these kids go for it?

Well, if she wanted to be a real leader, she couldn't ask what everyone wanted. She'd have to make the decision. If they didn't like the idea, she'd just have to make sure they did.

"We will divide into four groups and each group will brainstorm ideas," Ivy spoke with as much conviction as she could. She almost asked if everyone was okay with the idea, but caught herself just in time. A leader didn't ask, they led. "Each group will have a leader, who will present the group's best ideas when we all get together again."

Benjamin nodded at her and started dividing everyone up. Amber looked surprised, but also nodded to her. Kammie had frozen at the easel.

"You can do it, Kam," Ivy reassured her. "You'll be doing the exact same thing, just write down what they say and then let me know the best ideas."

Kammie swallowed hard, but finally nodded.

Then Ivy turned to Wren. Who did not nod. Wren did not look like she was in a nodding mood at all. It might be one of those times Wren turned into lightening, judging from her glare. As Kammie and Amber selected groups, Ivy turned a questioning look to Wren.

"What are you even doing?" Wren fumed.

"I'm leading the discussion. You'll be fine," Ivy soothed. Last thing she needed right now was one of Wren's explosions. "I know writing stuff down is one of your weaknesses, so just pick someone else to do it. You can do it."

"I'm not scared," Wren snorted. "You don't have to reassure me. That's not the point. The point is you didn't even ask us or anything. You just made the decision."

"Of course I did," Ivy snapped. "If you remember, you guys ran away. Somebody had to take charge. Now please, I'm sorry I didn't clear it with you first but there wasn't time. Will you please go be part of your group?"

Wren looked like she might yell some words that didn't belong in a library, or stomp off. But to Ivy's surprise, she took a deep breath, pursed her mouth, and turned to walk towards a group of waiting kids. Ivy watched her go. Wren was right, she had volunteered her friends again without consulting them. She'd have to work on that.

"I was thinking," Benjamin interrupted her thoughts. "I think Gail should lead one of the groups instead of you."

Ivy blinked. "What? Why?"

"That way you and I can talk," he waved Gail over. "Hey, can you take that last group?"

"I'm just an impartial observer tonight Ben," She shook her head. "Only here to record the proceedings for the paper. A good journalist never influences what she's reporting on. I have no opinions on the subject."

"Gimme a break, Gail," Benjamin smirked. "Since when have you ever not had opinions? Besides, you can run the group however you want, and I know you like to be in charge."

"I guess I could get a more in depth look," Gail nodded

thoughtfully. "Go undercover!"

Gail walked towards her group without any more protest.

"You sure turned that around quickly," Ivy said, impressed.

Benjamin shrugged. "Look, I wanted to apologize again for springing this on you guys. I didn't mean to. But I'm impressed by how you were able to step up."

"Thanks," Ivy wondered if Dr. Kim would be proud of her, too. "You know, the other Renegades are great too. They've just... they're still working on their weaknesses. They'll get there, every one of them. Don't hold it against them. Especially Kammie. She just doesn't transition well."

"Everyone is working on something," Benjamin smiled. "That's not a weakness, it's just being human. You'll be surprised at how much of a change you'll all go through between now and high school. But everybody has something to bring to the table. It's just not always what you expec—"

Loud laughter from Wren's group interrupted them. Ivy's head shot up. Were they laughing at Wren? Wren could do stupid things when she was angry, but Ivy wouldn't stand for anyone laughing at her. To her surprise, though, the kids seemed to be laughing WITH Wren. Actually, they all seemed to be having a great time. Huh. Interesting.

Nearby, Kammie handed out paper and pencil to her group. That seemed like the reverse of what she should be doing. Maybe Ivy would have to go help Kammie out when she finished talking with Benjamin. Amber looked like she'd assigned Afsheen to write down ideas. Gail, on the other hand, had commandeered the art easel, pulled a fresh piece of paper over it, and was pointing to each person in her group in turn. Round robin. It made more sense with a smaller group.

"I guess it's working out," Ivy shrugged. She'd been talking to herself but Benjamin nodded.

"It usually does," he replied, "one way or another."

Ivy checked in on Kammie's group, and was surprised to see them collecting the papers and reading them to each other. They seemed to be discussing the ideas. Ivy decided to let it go. It was almost time to bring everyone back together anyway.

"Five minutes," Ivy called out. "Then we'll get back together and every group can present their best idea or two."

Since each group had already narrowed down their ideas to just the best ones, they should all be ideas that would work. Hopefully Benjamin and the council could just take them straight to Principal Sophie.

"Hey, that was actually kind of fun," Wren chirped as they regrouped. "I think everyone enjoyed it. You know what? I make a pretty good leader."

Ivy didn't say anything. She was glad Wren had a successful group, but being funny for a few minutes and being a good leader were different things. Wren was a smart, energetic person, but realistically Ivy wasn't sure her raw, unfocused power would convert well to being the central processing unit in a group, and Ivy didn't want her to get hurt. People could be really mean to Wren.

"My group didn't really feel comfortable at first," Kammie said quietly. "But then I thought maybe everyone could write an idea or two down on paper, and we could talk about them anonymously. You know, take the pressure off. It worked really well. Our favorite idea was to maybe find a way to help kids discover what they're good at. Like some kind of quiz or something."

That was all Kammie said, but Ivy beamed at her. It was an amazing accomplishment for Kammie to talk to a crowd at all. Ivy even felt a little proud of herself for pushing the quiet girl out of her comfort zone just a little. Kammie returned to her group, and one of the other kids patted her on the back.

Gail stood and pointed to one idea written down on the easel. It had a big red circle around it.

"We came up with a lot of great ideas," she said. "But ended up with this one. We could get the teachers involved, to talk about careers and business involved with whatever subject they teach. Like jobs people can get if they're good at art, or how math affects things like calculating profit or even how many school newspapers we print, stuff like that."

"Or the carbon footprint of different industries!" Amber added. A lot of the kids agreed.

Amber stood and replaced Gail at the front of the room. Her group's idea was to bring in guest speakers from the community.

"But not just in fancy jobs," Amber emphasized. "In all kinds of jobs. I can ask Jewels, my boss at the clothing boutique, if she'd come in. Hey Ivy, maybe you could invite the author of that book you like so much. Doesn't she run some kind of company?"

Dr. Kim? She just ran one of the biggest robotics companies around. But invite Caroline Kim herself to speak at school? Ivy could never do that, could she? The idea grew quickly in Ivy's head. What if she did? And what if she could meet Caroline in person?

"Maybe," Ivy nodded. She pretended to be casual, but inside, her mind started to race with possibilities. What if it actually happened? Ivy was so lost in thought she almost didn't hear Wren's group's idea.

"So we thought it would be really fun," Wren's eyes blazed with excitement. "If we had some kind of business fair. You know, like a science fair, but with businesses. Like kids could work in groups and start their own little companies. What did you call a person who starts their own company, Tyrone?"

"An entrepreneur," he offered.

"Oh my gosh," gushed Afsheen, "that would be so fun!"

The room buzzed with excitement. Even Benjamin perked up. But Ivy's mind was wrapped up in how to word an email to Caroline.

What could she say that the great Dr. Caroline Kim, CEO of Sapai Industries, would even take the time to read?

7
THE LOVELACE GAZETTE

*T*he front page of *the Lovelace Gazette*.
It wasn't the first time Ivy had been on there, but this time she was alone in the photo. Or, at least, just her and Benjamin.

Gail's photo of the two of them shaking hands, along with an article about the Career Week kickoff, had appeared on the front page of the online version of the school newspaper on Wednesday. And by the time the printed copies of the paper came out on Thursday, word had already gotten out.

Axel Andrews, a girl with a perky blonde ponytail, flopped a copy of the paper on Ivy's desk during their math class. Somehow, she'd gotten her hands on a copy early. Ivy assumed it was because Axel wrote an events column called *Axel About Town* for the paper.

Axel had been a fairly popular kid among the other kids in their grade until the beginning of the sixth-grade year, when the Renegades had caught her stealing the election results they'd been accused of taking. Since then, Axel had been trying to fix her reputation, to find the right place to use her energy.

"I see you've been busy," Axel pointed to the front page. "Good job. I've never been on the front page, and now you've had your picture there twice."

Ivy gazed at the paper. The angle of the picture showed her whole face and only the back of Benjamin's head and his ear, but it was an ear everyone at school would recognize. The article didn't talk much about the brainstorming session. It focused on the results.

"Looks like Benjamin got the sign-off from Principal Sophie for all our ideas," Ivy read. "That's great. It should be a fun week."

Axel sighed. "How do you do it? I mean, I'm not allowed at student council events after the whole mix-up with the elections, but even so, I've been trying to get on the front page forever. What's your secret?"

"Good timing?" Ivy shrugged, not mentioning how much trouble the *mix-up* had caused them.

"Your good timing is going to open some serious doors for you, Ivy Rose," Axel leaned against her desk. "I wish I had some of that luck."

Axel was a complicated person. Ivy respected her strong drive. She was like a battery full of electrical charge. But what charged that battery was a thirst for recognition. Ivy appreciated wanting to get credit for the work you put into something, but sometimes with Axel, seeking that recognition became a goal in itself. Axel's yearning to be on the student council or get on the front page of the paper was so strong, it overpowered her logic circuits sometimes.

Ivy shrugged. "It's not that big of a deal. It's just a photo."

"Maybe so." Axel brought the paper to her own desk. "It just depends on what you do with it. And who sees it."

Who would see it? It's just a school newspaper. Nobody besides the students really cared. Ivy was more interested in the article, which explained how the whole Career Week was starting to shape up.

Ivy might not be able to help with more than a brainstorm, but she did plan on emailing Dr. Kim on the off-chance she might be willing to come speak. Maybe Ivy would send a link to the online copy of the article. That would explain the whole event better than Ivy ever could. The easy solution is sometimes the best. Besides, it wasn't like Dr. Kim would actually read the email. She probably had assistants to do that for her.

Wouldn't it be great if she did, though? Maybe she'd even see a younger version of herself in Ivy. A confident girl willing to step up. A girl with a plan for success. Who knows, maybe she'd even reply.

Ivy smiled to herself as she opened her math book.

"You're on the front page!" Wren waved the paper in Ivy's face. "That's so cool!"

They'd snagged a copy at lunch, and now all the Renegades were oohing and aahing over the photo. Ivy looked at it again. It really was a good photo. She looked so grown-up standing there with Benjamin. Serious and strong.

Dr. Kim had pointed out in at least three different chapters of *Success Plan* that you should grab every opportunity to contribute, and be bold about it. You never knew what path the smallest of actions could take you down.

"So they're going ahead with the science fair idea," Amber read. "Fantastic! That was my favorite of all the ideas we came up with. Benjamin named it the Entrepreneur Expo."

"We totally have to enter. Let's make a business." Wren jumped off the picnic table and bounced in front of them. "We already have experience from our spy business. And kids who do the Expo get a special pass for work time in the library. We could skip a bunch of classes."

Kammie shook her head. "That's not the purpose of in-school work time, Wren. It's supposed to be so everyone can join in, even if you can't meet after school. It's a special project. Everyone has to report to a sponsor to show how they use the time to learn stuff."

Kammie pointed to a place near the end of the article.

"Bah," Wren blew a raspberry. "I didn't read that far. Still, it's a lot better than sitting in a dumb stinky classroom."

Ivy had missed that detail too. She took the paper and read it more closely.

Wren continued to bubble with excitement. "What

kind of business are we going to make? Another spy business?"

Kammie shook her head. "Oh no. Didn't we learn anything from last time? No more spy stuff."

"Hey, there aren't any prizes or trophies or anything," Ivy finished the article and surrendered the paper to Wren's outstretched hands. "I like the idea of making a business, but if we aren't actually making any money, and it's not a competition, what's the point?"

"To get out of class," Wren gaped at her. "We already covered that. Keep up."

Amber laughed. "The point is to learn about businesses and what it's like to start your own. It says there's even a pretend permit process. You have to get a license to be in the Expo by filling out an application explaining your business idea, and get a different permit for your table space in the actual show."

"See?" Kammie declared. "Educational! We have to really think about our idea from all sides. You just can't get that kind of education from a lecture."

Ivy wasn't convinced. "I'm all for learning about businesses, especially since I hope to have my own one day in real life, but... this Expo sounds like a lot of work for nothing. I've got so much other stuff going on. The basketball team is depending on me. We're doing really well this season and I'm a key player. Plus I have homework for my electronics class and that big report for Mr. Vincent's English class. I just don't know if I can take on something new."

Wren put her hands on her hips and glared at Ivy. "Just because there's not some dumb trophy doesn't mean it's for nothing. Wait... You're doing extra homework? For something that's not even school? What?"

"My electronics class through TechAlive. It's not hard, but I have to keep my skills sharp somehow since we don't learn anything about electronics in school. Plus, it's fun." Ivy shrugged.

"You have a weird idea of fun, lady," Wren scoffed. "Anyway, the Expo will be easier than actual class, and we can use our club time, too. Come on... it'll be fun! Real fun, not like some stupid extra homework idea of fun. What could possibly go wrong?"

Ivy smirked at her.

"Stop saying that," Amber groaned. "But, I mean, if it's mostly in-school and club time, I can work around my Hebrew classes and internship. What about you Kammie?"

"I think it would be fun," Kammie said. "Though when the baby comes, I don't know how much I'll need to help out at home."

Ivy, Wren, and Amber froze. A chunk of bagel fell unnoticed from Wren's hand as they all stared at Kammie.

"Baby?" Amber squealed. "Baby? What baby?"

"I've been trying to tell you guys." Kammie blushed. "I'm going to have a little brother. So, I'm going to be extra busy pretty soon. Probably. I'm not sure what to expect."

Ivy's head spun. A baby? They'd just seen her mom. She sure didn't look pregnant. And why hadn't Kammie told her?

"I don't understand," Ivy said. Kammie might not have heard her over the squeals coming from Amber and the questions pelted at her from Wren.

Everyone quieted down as soon as Kammie's gentle voice explained. "Mom and Dad have been trying to have another kid for years. Dad's been trying to get Mom to adopt, and she's been dead set against it. But then Dad forwarded her this news link about the huge number of orphans in India. So a few years ago they started talking with this agency. We finally got matched to a little boy. I wasn't supposed to say anything because it could all fall apart, but Mom flies out next week to pick up my new brother. She'll be gone for a few weeks. I'm going to have to help Dad around the house, so, you know what that's like, Ivy. I may not have as much time as usual anymore."

Ivy was speechless. Just like that? Kammie was so reliable, always around. She'd always been available to talk, or hang out, or give her a ride.

"That's," Ivy tried to find the right words, "that's great. Isn't it? How do you feel about it?"

Kammie shrugged. "I have no idea. I mean, it's exciting but, I guess I'm nervous."

Amber squeezed Kammie hard. "Anytime you need help, you just ask me."

"I thought you were super busy," Wren pointed out.

"Baby, Wren! Didn't you hear her? Baby!"

Kammie began to squirm. "Can we talk about something else? I mean, something might go wrong when Mom goes out there, who knows. Anything could happen. I don't want to jinx it."

"Okay," Wren offered. "Let's talk business!"

"Dr. Kim does say to leverage all your chances to learn," Ivy replied. "But I just don't have a lot of mental energy to start a whole business."

"Tell you what, not only do I have the most time, I've also evidently been ignoring my true inner calling as a leader. I will be our CEO. Don't worry, I'll take care of everything!" Wren crackled with electricity. Ivy could almost feel it, almost smell the ozone even though she knew it was just her imagination. Wren had become lightening again.

Ivy looked away. Wren was many great things, but a natural born leader was not one of them. She was too disorganized and chaotic.

But it wasn't important. There weren't any trophies, no prizes. No winners. As long as they got a good grade, it didn't matter if they didn't succeed.

There was no reason not to let Wren give it a try. Even if it all fell apart, there weren't any consequences. After all, as Wren herself had pointed out, what could possibly go wrong?

8

THE GREENHOUSE

Sun warmed the south-facing front of a little blue Victorian house in the middle of the city. People often thought of Victorians as gigantic, sprawling structures with lacy ornamental trim dripping from every window, and San Francisco had lots of houses like that. But huddled between the towering modern condos and apartment buildings and the historic grand Victorian mansions were houses made at the turn of the century for everyday folks. Small homes with small rooms and large yards for the family's livestock. When big kitchens and indoor bathrooms became commonplace, they were awkwardly added to the houses wherever they would fit. Basements were converted into garages for modern cars, with sloped driveways leading down from the street.

Wren's little blue Victorian house was one of those.

Kammie's SUV slid into Wren's sloped driveway on Saturday. The door opened, and Kammie and Ivy spilled out onto the wide sidewalk, basking in the winter sun. They waved to Kammie's dad as he drove off.

"I love the warm winters here," Kammie closed her eyes and turned to face the sun like a flower.

The Renegades all had keys to Wren's side gate, which opened onto a narrow side yard which led from the street all the way into the backyard where their workshop, the Greenhouse, sat.

Today, though, Wren had told them all to come through the house.

"Welcome!" Wren kicked aside a few empty cardboard boxes on the floor. "The side gate is broken again, and mom's been too busy with Trixie to fix it. Amber's already in the Greenhouse, come on through."

They followed the long, messy, dark hallway to the bright kitchen at the end where Wren's little sister Trixie sat with her mom, squinting at an open book. Their dad scrubbed dishes at the sink.

"Hello, tinkerers!" Wren's mom greeted them. "Got big plans for the day?"

Trixie didn't look up from her book. "SHHHHHHH-HHHHHH! Go away."

Wren ruffled Trixie's hair. The younger girl batted her hand away and continued to glare at the book.

"Hello, Mrs. Sterling," Kammie said politely. "Mr. Sterling. Hello Trixie."

Everyone nodded at her.

"Have a great time." Wren's mom turned back to

Trixie. "How about this one, honey. What does this word say?"

Ivy and Kammie followed Wren out the sliding glass door to a backyard. The wisteria vine growing all over the Greenhouse was ropy and naked for the winter. Since the little building's front wall and most of the roof were glass, Ivy could see their two work tables inside, covered in tiny off-cuts of cardboard and various tools. Behind them, a mishmash of bins and random objects packed the back wall's floor to ceiling shelves. Amber sat on a stool inside reading the latest *Sarah and Simon* spy book.

Ivy's whole body relaxed. No matter how busy her life was, the Greenhouse always felt like a haven. A place to try new things and make mistakes. There was no winning in the Greenhouse. Nothing she needed to prove. Only making, doing, and investigating.

The door creaked as Ivy shoved her way through the wisteria and into the Greenhouse. Inside, it smelled like cardboard, sunlight, and hot glue. She sat and kicked her feet up on the folding table. Amber set her book aside.

"I'm gonna have to spend a lot of today working on my math homework, sorry." Ivy flopped some paper on the table next to her feet. "I've got a game tonight right in the middle of when I usually do it."

"Yeah," Amber nodded. "I had to put in an extra day at my internship this week. Bygone is clearing out this rich old lady's closet, and it's a lot of stuff to go through. Maybe we can just pull out the microscope. Do something mellow."

The microscope, a gift from Amber's Uncle Tim when his microbiology lab upgraded, was the pride of the club. But at the beginning of the school year, the double magnification eyepieces broke in an accident. Now it languished under a dusty cover, rarely used.

Ivy still blamed herself for that, six or seven months later. She should have been able to stop it. She had seen tempers escalating between Wren and her sister like energy building up before an explosion. She'd tried to calm things down, but hadn't been able to defuse the situation. She hadn't been a good enough leader. The double magnification eyepieces had shattered in their resulting tussle.

Still, it could have been worse. The microscope still worked, but without double magnification, it wasn't the same. And now, every use was tinged with guilt and failure.

Ivy didn't want to think about the microscope, so she changed the subject. "Hey, is Trixie joining us today?"

Ivy glanced through the windows into the kitchen. Trixie still sat at the table with her mom. She was crying.

"I don't think so. Trixie's having a really hard time learning to read. Mom's trying to help but, well, Mom really isn't a very good teacher. She's not very patient."

"I don't remember when I learned to read," Amber sat on the stool across from Ivy. "Maybe 5? 6? Same age as Trixie, but she seems so young."

"Apparently she's behind the other kids," Wren shrugged. "She can't even get the kindergarten words they're learning. She talked late, and she caught up with that so I guess she'll catch up with reading too. I feel bad for her. I was all blah, blah, blah way too early, but I was also all read, read, read really early too. I would have melted into goo before I met you guys if I couldn't read."

"Maybe she just needs more time," Amber suggested.

Wren looked through the windows as her mom rubbed her sister's back. "Maybe, but I feel bad for her. I love reading. And writing, too. Words come out of my mouth too fast, and even completely out of order, too. And then everyone's like whoa, why the heck did you say that? But writing slows my brain down. I can get the words mostly in an order other people don't freak out about. But Trix can't do that."

"Yet," added Amber.

"Yet." Wren crossed her fingers.

"She'll be fine. She just needs to buckle down and focus." Ivy spread her math homework on the table in front of her. "I know how that feels. It's so hard to organize my time these days."

The others nodded. Suddenly, Amber dug into her bag and pulled out a small, shimmering notebook.

"I know!" She waved it at them. "We can make BuJos! That's our quick and easy project for today. The fashion contest would have killed me without mine."

"A who joe what?" Wren lifted an eyebrow in confusion.

"A BuJo," Amber clarified unhelpfully. "A bullet journal. Look."

She flipped the notebook open. The pages were filled

with random lists, drawings, calendars, and colorful washi tape.

"I have a bunch of lists too," Wren said as she paged through the journal. "Lists everywhere! On little pieces of paper, in some random notebook, I accidentally put one in the fridge once. Then I start doodling on them and suddenly cats are riding dragons all over assignments for Mr. Vincent's class. And I forget to check stuff off, and then I write new lists and they get lost too. Lists multiply like dastardly little rabbits."

"I like lists." Kammie looked over Wren's shoulder at the notebook. "I have these special notepads that are long and skinny, made just for lists. I keep one by my bed, and if I start thinking too much at night and can't sleep, I write down all the stuff I need to do."

"That's a good idea," agreed Wren.

Kammie nodded. "It helps quiet my brain. Once I write it down, I know I won't forget. Then I can fall asleep."

"This is a whole system," Amber explained. "Like a planner and a to-do list and a journal all in one. You put in whatever kind of organization tool you need. And you can make it really fancy or simple, whatever you want. I use mine to doodle sometimes, too. It was invented by a guy named Ryder Carroll. Isn't this one pretty?"

The inside was pretty too. All the lettering swirled with tidy flourishes. Colorful sketches decorated pages next to calendars that seem to be thrown in at random.

"It doesn't seem very organized for an organization system," Ivy frowned.

"Ah but it is," Amber replied. "I'll show you. Do we have any notebooks? We just need a notebook and a pen to get started."

Wren yanked a bin labeled "PAPERY THINGS" off the shelf. Inside were sheets of lined and plain paper of all different colors. Some were heavy and stiff, like cardstock, and some were light like tissue paper. Various notebooks emerged, too. Most had been saved from the trash, the used pages ripped out and recycled. Wren found three spiral notebooks with a bunch of pages left in each. She handed one to Kammie, one to Ivy, and kept one herself.

Amber flipped to her first page. It said INDEX at the top, and listed a bunch of page numbers. "Give yourself a couple of pages in the front to be your index, and then number all the other pages. You can number as you go, or do them all up front, or do just the odds or even pages."

Kammie began diligently numbering every page in her notebook. Wren groaned.

"What's next?" she asked, impatiently watching Kammie.

"It's a good idea to use another page in the front for a key." Amber showed them her third page, which had a bunch of symbols, all labeled. "Not everyone has them, it's really the Index that's the most important, but I like including a key. It reminds me what symbols I'm using for things like events versus tasks or appointments, completing tasks, moving a task to a new to-do list, stuff like that."

"And after that?" Wren pressed. "What do you use these symbols on?"

"Whatever you want! What's most helpful for you? Some people make Future Logs, which is an overview of the next six months on two pages. Just divide each page into three equal sections, so you have six total, and label them for each of the next six months. Then go back and write down the page numbers in your index." Amber turned to her index and pointed to *Future Log: pg 5-6*. "Write down anything you have going on that month, like a doctor's appointment or if you're going on a trip."

"That's not a lot of space for everything I have to do in a month," Ivy said.

"Well, it's supposed to just be the really important stuff. And it's small on purpose, so you don't overschedule. For all the little stuff, like homework assignments, and your practices and games, you can make a separate weekly calendar, a to-do list if you want. Or you can make the week or a whole month on a page or spread over two pages. You can adapt it to whatever you, specifically, need."

"I need a lot of to-do lists and calendars for what days I have practice and class, and my chores at home," Ivy said.

"I just need lists for my assignments and stuff, and a place to draw that isn't homework I have to turn in." Wren began to draw spirals on her unfinished Index page.

"I like calendars, and weekly assignments, and would love a place to put recipes and ideas," Kammie added.

"Perfect," Amber replied. "Just draw a new calendar where you want, and how big you want, and put the page number in your index. Or your weekly list... and put the page number in the index. My future log gives me an overview of the long term stuff. Like here, I have the date school gets out for summer. That would get lost in a weekly calendar since it's a few months away still. As long as you record everything in the index, you'll always know where to find it. I even put my art in the index."

"What do these symbols mean?" Kammie pointed to one of Amber's to-do lists. "Are they in your key?"

"Yeah, when you make a new to-do list, you migrate the old one." Amber turned the book so they could see. "That just means you rewrite the list whenever you need to update it. These are my symbols for if I finished a task, or moved it to the next list or to a different month, or if I decided to get rid of the task entirely."

"And those are the same symbols you put in your key, right?" Kammie asked.

"Yup," Amber nodded. "You can find all kinds of ideas for BuJos online. Tons and tons of people use them. Some are really creative! Seriously, this little journal is a lifesaver when it comes to organizing a busy day."

"My handwriting isn't very nice, though." Wren ran her hand over the journal.

"That doesn't matter," Amber shrugged. "I mean, it's just for you, no one else has to see it. You can make it as fancy or messy as you want, as long as it's functional."

Wren picked up her spiral notebook and a pen. "It's worth a try."

BULLET JOURNAL

MATERIALS
- 1 notebook, old or new, or a binder and paper
- Pens, pencils, and/or markers

Make a Key
- ☐ - task
- ○ - event/holiday
- △ - appointment
- ◇ - practice/game
- ! - deadline/due date
- ✓ - completed
- > - migrated

Make an Index

Label the first page or two of your journal INDEX, and number the pages. Write the name and page number of each new entry in here when you create it

Do a To-Do

Make a new To-Do list often! Check off completed tasks and decide if unfinished ones are still important. If so move, or MIGRATE them to the new list

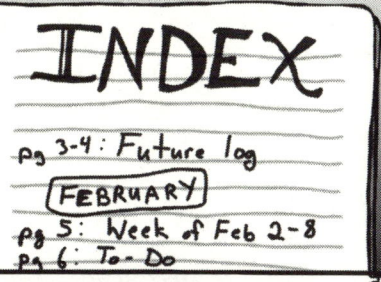

Try A Future Log

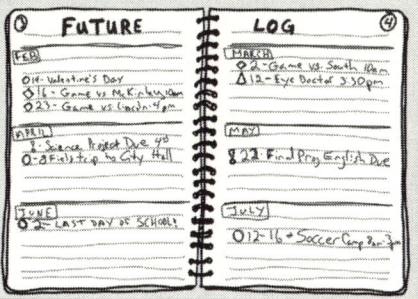

Divide two facing pages into three rows each, and label the rows with the names of the next six months

WHAT ELSE WOULD HELP YOU STAY ORGANIZED?
Lists of shows? Menus? Weekly calendars? Put it in there! The internet has lots of great ideas, too

9

RENEGADE ENTREPRENEUR BUSINESS, OR REB FOR SHORT

"This meeting of Renegade Entrepreneur Business-ness will now come to order!" Wren slammed her lunchbox down on the picnic table, startling Kammie and Amber. "We'll call it REB for short."

Ivy didn't look up from her book. "That's a terrible name, Wren."

The school hadn't officially announced the Entrepreneur Expo, but at Sunday's basketball game, Emma said she heard they'd announce it this week. It was only going to be open to middle school students. At least that's what Emma said, and who knew if she actually knew anything.

"It's just a working title," Wren said. "To throw competitors off track."

Ivy chuckled.

"Are we starting the business already?" Kammie moaned. "Shouldn't we wait until they announce it?"

Wren ripped off a chunk of bagel and stuffed it in her mouth, talking around it. "No way. I want our company to be the best! So we have to get started now. I even read some stuff on public speaking. I meant to look up how to be a CEO, but got sidetracked, but it turned out okay because I'm following the other advice. Look! I wrote down some jokes to warm up the crowd. You're the crowd."

She shuffled through a small, disorderly pile of index cards, selected one and squinted at her own messy writing.

"Hello and welcome everyone," Wren read slowly. "What did the dog say when he walked into a bar... no, wait. Bag? No, I was right. Bar. It definitely says bar. What did the dog say when he walked into a bar?"

She looked up expectantly. Amber shrugged and twisted the top off her thermos. Kammie looked away.

"Aww come on you guys," Wren whined. "What did the dog say when he walked into a bar? He said..." She squinted at the card again. "He said to the bartender 'you're very fetching.'"

Ivy looked up from her book, "What does that mean?"

"I... I don't know," Wren shook her head. "That's a dumb joke. Maybe I have a better one, hang on."

Ivy sighed, turning back to her sandwich and book as Wren began rifling through her card stack again. Finally, Wren pulled out another card.

"Here we go," she held the card aloft. "This one's funny! Why don't oysters donate to charity? Because they're shellfish. Get it? SHELLFISH!"

No one laughed.

"Oh come on you guys, that was at least a little funny," Wren pouted.

"Why are you telling jokes at all?" Ivy asked. "What's even going on here?"

Wren's shoulders slumped. She pushed aside her lunchbox and sat on the edge of the picnic table. "I'm trying to be a good leader. I even have talking points. Hang on."

She dug into her pocket and pulled out a different stack of wrinkled cards. She looked at the joke cards with regret and tried to stuff them into her other pocket, but a few fell out. Ivy reached down to grab them before they blew away. Amber and Kammie started talking about an English assignment.

"Okay, okay you guys," Wren looked up in desperation. "I've got this. We're gonna be the best company in the school. See? I wrote it down. It's our goal. It says *Be The Best Company*. We need to have asserts. Wait, that says assets. And labels. Liables? What does that mean?"

"Liabilities and assets?" Ivy offered. "Look, we don't need to talk about this stuff right now. The first thing you need to do when forming a business is figure out the structure. What your business actually is."

Wren glared at her. "I've got it under control, Ivy. I'm the CEO, remember? We said I could be the leader. So let me lead. What's this say?"

Ivy sighed as she looked up from her book again and tried to make out the writing on the card. "Ummm. I think it says gross profits."

Wren turned the card back around so she could see it and squinted. "GROSS profits? Why did I write that? Aren't profits good? What's gross about making money?"

"That's just a kind of profit. I was just reading about it yesterday." Ivy waved *Success Plan* at them. "Profit is the money you make from your business, right? So all the money you make is called *revenue*. *Gross profit* is how much you make after you take out the cost you paid for what you sold. Then *net profit* is how much you make after you pay for stuff like rent and worker's salaries and business taxes and stuff. Like if you sell a sandwich for two dollars, then two dollars is your *revenue*. But if the bread and ham and mayo cost you one dollar, then you actually only made one dollar, right? That one dollar you made is your *gross profit*."

"I'm not sure I follow you. That's really confusing," Wren squeezed her eyes shut. "But two dollars is a great price for a sandwich."

Amber and Kammie laughed, but Ivy turned back to her book.

"Okay, I'll figure it out," Wren brushed her chin length hair out of her eyes. It immediately fell back in front of them. "Maybe Ivy's right, the first thing we should do is figure out what kind of business this is. Oh! Wait! I have another idea for a name..."

"Does it have 'cat' in it?" Amber smirked.

Wren paused and turned to her with an open mouth, "How did you know?!?"

"Lucky guess," Amber chuckled.

"You're good," Wren patted her head. "The most important part of a business is the name, after all."

Everyone laughed except Ivy. This was going to be a disaster if Wren didn't stop messing around. Maybe she could help.

"The name is just like a coat of paint that makes a business look pretty. We have to figure out the basic foundation of the business first, just like if we were building something. You have to plan first and make a strong foundation," Ivy set aside her book. "Like what are we going to DO? Sell lemonade? Do creative jobs for people? Wash cars? Become therapists? If you're going to be a CEO, you have to figure out what the business even is."

"That makes sense," Wren fished a pencil out of her pocket and scribbled on one of the cards. "So what do we want to do?"

"I liked inventing spy gear," Amber offered.

Kammie shook her head. "No more spy stuff. Come on. We got in so much trouble."

"But we were pretty successful for a while," Wren pointed out. "We should probably be an invention company of some kind. Oh! How about Inventor Cats! Feline-a-ventors? No, I've got it! Cat Workshop."

"We're not making cats!" Ivy frowned. "This has nothing to do with cats!"

"Yet!" Wren added with a mischievous smile.

Amber doubled over with laughter. Even Kammie laughed out loud. Ivy forced a smile, reminding herself again that it didn't matter.

Poor Wren. She was having a harder time than Ivy had expected. There must be some way to help. The other three were rolling with laughter about more of Wren's jokes. Real jokes at least. The fact that they were having a great time was wonderful, but it wasn't action. Wren needed some real power to make the business work.

Ivy looked down at *Success Plan*. Dr. Kim had power. Ivy had already read the entire book twice. There were so many sparks of wisdom, so much helpful advice. It was the best non-fiction book Ivy had ever read. It inspired her, filled her with hope.

That's what Wren needed. A little jump-start from a powerful engine. The book could be her jumper cables.

Ivy caressed the cover. She hadn't let it out of her sight since she got it, but Wren needed help. Ivy closed her eyes and turned away from the others as she hugged the book, so they wouldn't see.

Then she took a deep breath and turned back to Wren, who was gasping for breath between laughs.

"Hey," Ivy cleared her throat. "Do you want to borrow *Success Plan*? Dr. Kim is a genius. She's created a bunch of successful companies. It might give you some great ideas."

Wren looked at the book in Ivy's outstretched hand. She shrugged and grabbed it. "Sure, why not? Thanks."

She shoved the book into the outside pocket of her lunch bag, the corner creasing. Ivy cringed.

Suddenly her cell phone buzzed. It was probably an incoming email or text from her mom. Ivy usually kept her phone in her backpack or pocket, following school rules.

She almost never pulled it out during the day. But as Wren tossed the lunch bag back on the table, book side down, Ivy pulled it out.

She needed a distraction.

It was an email.

Curious, Ivy clicked open her mail app. And froze.

It was from Caroline Kim herself. At least that's what it said in the FROM line. Right there. An email from THE Dr. Caroline Kim. Right there in her own mailbox. The subject line said "Sounds great, see you there."

Ivy blinked, then opened the email.

10

EMAIL

"*Dear Ms. Park,*" the email began. "*Thank you for contacting me about your school event. And thank you for including a link to the article in your school paper. The girl in the photo reminds me of myself. I truly believe that strong girls are the hope for our future. I would be happy to come speak at your school, please have your coordinator contact my office to arrange details. If all the Lovelace students are as determined as the young woman in the photo, the event will be a big success. I will also attend the Entrepreneur Expo. What a wonderful idea! I look forward to meeting all the entrepreneurs and hearing about their wonderful business ideas. Best Regards, Caroline.*"

A rushing noise buzzed through Ivy's head, drowning out her surroundings. She couldn't hear anything. Or see anything. Or think. It was too good to be true! She might meet Caroline Kim herself. And she'd signed the email with her first name.

She, Ivy Rose Park, was on a first name basis with Dr. Caroline Kim! And she'd been impressed by Ivy. Maybe Caroline really would become her mentor. She could get into any college with a letter of recommendation from Caroline Kim. Ivy could learn about electrical engineering and starting companies from an expert. From the inside.

From her mentor. Caroline.

The dream had seemed silly just moments ago, but now... could it actually happen? Why not? Suddenly everything seemed possible.

But, Ivy already had so many commitments. Her mom needed her. She needed to help with dinners and dishes and laundry. With Kammie's mom still gone, and that baby coming, she'd have to figure out rides to games.

And then there was basketball. Ivy loved playing. She loved the rush of competition and the physical exercise. She loved pushing her mind and body and reflexes. She was already better at dribbling with her left hand after all the drills. She made the winning basket at last weekend's game. Her team needed her. She couldn't let Emma and the others down.

Now the Expo. Caroline was going to be there. Ivy needed to start taking it more seriously. Would she be able to find the energy, as well as the time?

But it was an opportunity to run her own business. What if it was successful? What if, her mind started racing, what if her business was so good that it impressed Caroline?

A successful business at the Expo could be the catapult to truly becoming Caroline's protege. Then all Ivy's dreams might come true. Surely, THAT was something Ivy could make time for.

A snort of laughter brought Ivy back to the picnic table. Back to the warm sun, the oblivious kids swarming all over the playground equipment, buzzing like an overloaded circuit.

Kammie wiped away a tear of laughter, a huge smile covering her face. Amber's skin was pink from laughing. How long had Ivy spent thinking about that email?

"That was so much fun! Too bad we didn't get much done." Wren slung her lunch bag over her shoulder. *Success Plan* dangled precariously from its pocket.

A cold wave ran over Ivy.

Wren.

Wren might ruin everything. Ivy had already agreed to let Wren be CEO. She promised. And Wren was trying so hard. It wasn't her fault, being a leader was really hard. Not everyone was cut out for it, and that was okay. But with Wren in charge the business would be a disaster. What would Caroline think? She would laugh in Ivy's face.

Ivy's whole future was hanging on this business. Maybe Wren would read the book. Maybe she'd get inspired and turn out to be a great leader after all. With hope in her eyes, Ivy glanced at Wren's lunch bag where the book hung, forgotten.

"Hey Wren," Ivy choked. "Take care of my book okay? It's really good. You really should read it."

"What?" Wren checked on the book, shoving it deeper into the pocket to keep it from falling out. "Oh, sure, thanks, I'll read it when I get home."

Ivy hoped she would. Because they'd agreed that Wren was going to run this company. And there was nothing Ivy could do about it now.

11

IT'S OFFICIAL

The official rules of the Entrepreneur Expo were simple. Start a business, get the proper "permits," fill out some paperwork on how the business is set up and how it will be run, make any prototypes needed, and present everything in a booth at the Expo.

Any middle schooler could apply for a permit, basically just a permission slip from their teachers to take part in the Entrepreneur Expo. Applications had to include a company name, explain what the company did, how they were going to present it for the Expo, and a business plan. Each company needed to appoint a CEO and any other jobs. Then groups could meet in the library to work on their company whenever their teachers let them.

Permit applications were due on Friday, so kids who wanted to apply were allowed to work in the library after school that week.

"Geeze, this is as bad as homework! Whose dumb idea

was this?" Wren flopped a stack of papers on their library table. Then she flopped herself in a chair with the same enthusiasm.

All the Renegades pulled their chairs closer except Amber, whose face was hidden behind a book called *Hebrew For Your Bar/Bat Mitzvah*.

Kammie pulled a paper from the stack and began reading. Ivy read along over her shoulder. Wren was right, there was a lot to fill out.

"Well let's get to work," Ivy declared. "I need to be at the gym for basketball practice in like fifteen minutes."

"That isn't going to be enough time," Kammie turned over the page. The questions continued on the back. "This doesn't look simple."

"Don't worry, we've got you covered." Wren pulled out a pen and immediately started chewing on it. "You just come back when you're done and we'll fill you in. We're going to stay here until this whole stupid form is filled out. Amber, come on. Isn't it bad enough that Ivy's always reading?"

Amber glanced over the top of her book. "Shalom. Ma kore?"

Wren reached across the table and tried to push *Hebrew For Your Bar/Bat Mitzvah* into Amber's face, but could only scrape it with her fingertips. Amber stuck out her tongue and disappeared behind the pages again.

"Please Amber?" Wren groaned. "We have paperwork to fill out and you're one of our best filler-outers."

"I'm listening, you get started," Amber said from behind the book.

"What is that, anyway?" Wren asked.

"I'm studying for my Bat Mitzvah," Amber's book replied.

"Guys, I only have ten more minutes. Can we get started?" Ivy looked at the clock on her phone.

"Oh okay," Wren nodded. She tapped her pen on the table, looking over the first page. "Name of company. Uh-oh. They're starting with a hard one."

Ivy took a deep breath and slowly let it out. "Why don't we just skip ahead?"

"Good idea," Wren agreed. She skimmed the page, then flipped it over and skimmed the back. "Nope, these all look pretty hard. I mean, what is a corporate structure? And do we really have to make someone a secretary? Secretaries on tv just get people coffee, and we don't even drink coffee. Though Dad let me have some the other day, and it really wasn't too bad with enough cream and sugar in it. But it took a LOT of cream and sugar..."

"Can we not talk about coffee?" Ivy fidgeted and glanced at her phone again. "I think corporate structure usually means if your business is a non-profit or a regular company or something."

"No, that's on this page." Kammie waved the sheet she was reading.

"Hmm," Ivy mused. "Then maybe how we're going to divide up the tasks? Like who does what jobs, and who makes the decisions about stuff like money and other big stuff."

Wren peered at the paper. "That makes sense. Yeah, it says something like that here. I guess I missed it. Sometimes I miss stuff that's totally obvious, like this one time..."

Ivy glanced at her clock again as Wren rambled on. Ivy grabbed one of the other pages, ignoring Wren's long and probably pointless story. Another time she'd enjoy it, but not now.

The role of CEO, the Chief Executive Officer who made most of the decisions about a company, was specifically called out. Ivy remembered that Wren had immediately mentioned CEOs when she started talking about the Expo. How much of the process had come from Wren's brainstorm? Apparently, Wren's brainstorming group really thought about the idea before presenting it.

The Renegades had already chosen their CEO, so, on to the next question.

"If your company manufactures a product," The paper asked. "What is that product?"

Ivy got out a pencil. They'd already decided to invent stuff. But what were they going to make? Ivy tapped her lips with the eraser. Something really technical. Something that would impress Caroline. Sapai Industries was a robotics company. So, robots? Yes, inventing a robot would definitely impress Caroline! And everyone else, too.

Not only would it be impressive, but it was something their group could do, with Ivy handling the electronics,

Amber designing it, Kammie programming it, and Wren handling the mechanics like how the wheels and gears worked. They were the perfect team to make their own robot. And it used everyone's best skills. Wren might not be a natural leader but she was great at figuring out how different parts worked together to make something move or spin.

"That's it!" Ivy declared. "We can be a robotics company! It's perfect."

"I was right in the middle of a sentence," Wren frowned.

"Oh sorry, I have to go soon," Ivy explained. "You can keep talking about whatever you were saying when I head to practice but I wanted to help fill this stuff out while I'm here."

Everyone stared at Ivy. Had she missed something? Even Amber was staring at her. Then Ivy noticed the Hebrew book was already closed and pushed to the side. Had they all been talking? What had she missed?

"What?" she asked.

"We were just discussing potential names," Kammie explained. "Wren said we'd decide what sort of inventions to make after that. Weren't you listening?"

"I guess not," Ivy threw up her hands. "I'm just trying to help and I don't have a lot of time. I don't really care what we call it, I care what we DO."

The alarm on Ivy's phone went off. Great. Now she had to go. She grabbed her backpack, trying not to get upset. She reminded herself that she wasn't in charge.

"Look," Ivy told them. "I have to go. Think about it, okay? We should make robots."

"We'll put it on the list." Wren gave her a thumb's up. "Have a good practice!"

The other three turned back to their discussion as she walked out of the library. At the door, Ivy looked back over her shoulder. They weren't even watching her. The door closed with a click as Ivy raced down the quiet, empty hallway towards the gym across the street.

The other members of the team were already stretching on the court as Ivy ran past. She waved at Coach Bakes, who did not look happy, and tossed her backpack into her locker. She changed into her gym shoes and yanked a pinny over her head, sliding into place next to Emma. She started stretching.

"Dude," Emma whispered. "You're late!"

"I know," Ivy whispered back. "I was in a business meeting."

They both giggled at how weird that sounded. The coach blew a whistle and everyone jogged for the wire cage that held the balls.

"I'm doing that too," Emma spoke in a regular voice over the squeaking of sneakers on the court. "But my team is taking care of the paperwork. I don't have time to mess around with all the details."

Ivy passed her a ball as they lined up for layups.

"It's tough to balance," Ivy admitted. "I mean, it's not just time right? It's mental energy, too. You can't just leave for another commitment when you're the boss."

Emma nodded. "Though, when someone else is making the decisions, you just have to trust their choices, right?"

Ivy tried not to think about Wren's choices as she took a shot at the basket.

∼

"Welcome, sweaty one! You're back!" Wren smiled at Ivy. "We finished all the paperwork. I've never even gotten my homework done so fast. We make a great team. Glad you made it back before we took off."

Ivy paused, breathing heavily from running between the gym and the now-almost-deserted library. Outside, the evening had grown chilly and dark. She placed her backpack on top of the wide library table. Amber had her book out, and Kammie worked on some math.

"What did you decide to call it?" Ivy asked. "Robot-cat-topia?"

"That would have been AWESOME," Wren laughed. "But no. We aren't doing robots. We're going to make toys. But cool toys, stylish toys. We can do some electronic stuff in there too, but we decided not to make the business all techy like everyone else is gonna do. We want it to be fun! I have this great idea for some blocks."

Ivy froze. Toys? BLOCKS? That would never impress Caroline. She began to breathe a little faster.

"Blocks? Seriously?"

"Yeah, cool blocks, with these things on them," Wren

waved her hands around to demonstrate... something. When she saw Ivy's expression, her smile faltered. "I mean... Trust me. We all agreed. They'll be great."

Kammie and Amber nodded.

"It's a great idea," Amber agreed. "I'm so excited to work on the stuff we came up with. Wren, you really are so creative."

"It was a really fun brainstorm," Kammie added. "Especially when—"

"Right?!" Amber and Kammie giggled about something Ivy didn't understand.

Only Wren could see Ivy's expression.

"Blocks?" Cold fear gripped Ivy. Like all her energy shut off suddenly at the source. "Blocks? That's our business?"

"Yup, see you tomorrow," Amber glanced out the window to the street beyond. "My mom's here. I'm giving Kammie a ride. Are you ready?"

Kammie followed Amber out the door, with a last glance over her shoulder at Ivy. The library door closed behind her with a quiet thunk. Wren fidgeted with the stack of paperwork. Lines of neat, readable writing lined each page. Wren hoisted her backpack onto her shoulder and fiddled with the paperclip holding the pages together.

"Would you like to read it?" Wren held out the papers.

Ivy knew she should. She knew Wren meant well. She knew. But. All her hopes for her future, her dreams of seeing respect in Caroline's eyes, maybe even admiration, depended on having a killer presentation at the Expo. It would be her only chance, ever.

The only time she'd ever meet one of her heroes. The only chance she'd ever have to make her dreams come true by showing Caroline what she could do.

And they were making toy blocks.

Ivy grabbed her bag and stormed out, leaving Wren and her outstretched arm full of paperwork behind.

And feeling terrible about it.

12

BLOCKS

*E*xcited groups of kids swarmed into every corner of the library. Middle schoolers had signed up for the Expo in droves. They packed every table. Some even crowded into open spots on the floor. And they weren't quiet. The librarian kept moving stacks of books away from kids and hushing everyone. No one paid any attention.

For once, the noise didn't seem to bother Wren. She'd somehow snagged them a table, and flopped sheets of cardstock, a ruler, a pair of scissors, and some wooden blocks on it. The table was small, but they were lucky to have it. Wren pushed the scissors aside and added a pack of markers and some tape.

Emma and her group sat at a larger table nearby. Ivy recognized the five of them from her various classes: Axel, Tiffanie, Lily, Tyrone from student council, and Emma.

At another table, a group of six boys threw things at each other and talked loudly. Ivy recognized Milo Jones,

Wren's friend that Amber always acted weird around, and the curly blond hair of his best friend Bobby. Whenever the librarian scolded them, they'd get quiet, but as soon as she left, they'd start getting rowdy again. It was hard for the other groups to hear each other over them.

"Okay," Wren rubbed her hands together, somehow blocking out all the noise. "I know you're not sold on this idea, Ivy, but give it a chance. In my head, it's really awesome."

"I can't wait to see it," Ivy felt horrible about how she'd acted yesterday. She had to make it up to them.

But Ivy couldn't shake the cold fear that she would make a fool of herself in front of Caroline. She'd had a nightmare last night that Caroline laughed and laughed at her all night long. *Blocks,* her hero kept repeating, *blocks? Who cares about blocks?*

Ivy shook her head. It was just a stupid dream. Just her brain firing off random electricity leftover from the day. Playing her fears back like a movie. She needed to switch off the fear and switch on some problem solving. It was time to be on the team.

"Wait, what's the name of our company?" Ivy suddenly realized she didn't even know.

"We picked REBELs Incorporated," Kammie smiled. "It's an acronym. Each letter stands for a word."

"What words?" Ivy asked.

"Renegade Entrepreneur Business Expo League!" Kammie giggled. "That way we can still call ourselves the Renegades."

Ivy couldn't help but smile. "I like it. But are you sure we can't make a robot?"

Wren ignored her and held up one of the wooden blocks. "This is a block."

"Gosh, really?" Amber smirked.

"It's our GOAL, sort of." Wren spun the cube around. "I mean, it's what our goal looks like but not what it looks like."

"What?" Amber asked.

Wren replied but Ivy didn't hear her. Instead, Ivy's attention flickered over to Emma's table. Axel passed out folders. They all sat and listened to her talk. It looked so organized. Everyone looked interested. Ivy would have to ask Emma what was in the folders later.

Back at her own table, Wren set the block on the cardstock, then traced around it. The resulting drawing of a square was about an inch and a half on each side. She traced four more squares, for a total of five.

"I'm not sure how many I need," she explained. "But let's work with this. Okay, so we talked about toys for older kids..."

"And you came up with blocks?" Ivy chuckled.

"When you say it like that, I can see why you're confused," Amber shrugged. "You weren't there, but the path we followed to get to it made a lot of sense. Just listen."

Wren used the ruler to mark the middle of each side of each square. Then she measured a quarter inch, centered at each mark so each side of each square had a quarter inch area marked out at its center.

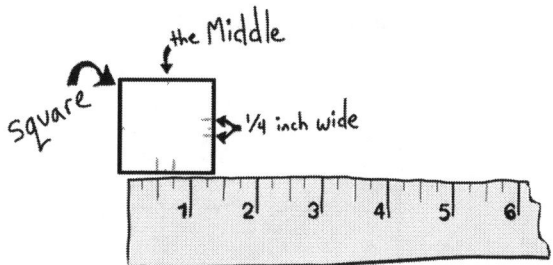

"We can draw lines connecting these marks in whatever kinds of patterns we want. It will make little paths between the edges. And if each side of the square has a path the same size in the same place," Wren reasoned, "then they'll match up no matter how we turn them."

"Okay, that's interesting," Ivy agreed. "But why?"

"Infinity cubes!" Wren began connecting the marks on the squares with quarter inch wide lines. "Like infinity tiles, but cubes."

On one square she connected opposite sides, so the square looked like it had a big cross on it. On another, she curved the lines, and on another, she connected them in a T shape, and added a little nub on the other side.

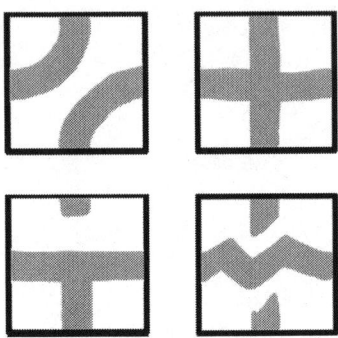

Suddenly, Ivy saw it. Any way she rotated or connected the squares, they would match up, creating one solid maze-like path.

"Now we just color them in with the markers," Wren explained.

"We should color them before cutting them out, so we don't get marker marks on the table," Kammie began to make more squares on another sheet of cardstock.

Amber selected a teal and a plum marker. The colors looked lovely together. She began to color in the background with the teal marker and the paths with the plum.

Ivy wasn't sure what they would do with these little squares, but it seemed simple enough. She grabbed some cardstock and made a few, too. Soon they had a bunch of squares of cardstock on the table, colored and cut out. Ivy started arranging them. No matter how she rotated or combined them, they always created a consistent pathway. It was soothing. She shuffled and reshuffled them, creating new patterns and color combinations.

"But these aren't blocks," Ivy pointed out.

"We can tape them together to make a cube. How many sides does a cube have?" Wren tugged off a piece of tape.

"Six," Kammie replied.

Wren taped four squares around a fifth, one attached to each side. Then she folded them up and hinged a sixth on like a lid. Then she made another cube the same way.

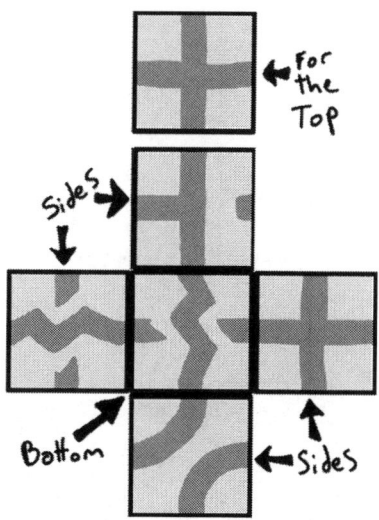

"Why don't we just glue the tiles to the wooden cube?" Amber asked. "It would be a lot easier."

"Because I only have two wooden cubes," Wren replied, showing them her two completed infinity cubes. "We have to make a ton of these."

Ivy could see the possibilities. A bunch of infinity cubes would be relaxing to play with. Ivy found herself twisting and turning the cubes, watching the changes in color, following the paths as they twisted along the faces of the cube, and then down the sides. Following the path from cube to cube. Kammie passed her another completed cube. With each additional cube, the possible ways to connect them and their resulting patterns grew.

"This is actually really soothing," Ivy admitted. "I still think a robot would be better, but I can see a bunch of these cubes as an actual product."

"See?" Wren grinned. "But tapping all the sides together looks weird. Maybe we can figure out how to fold them instead."

"What does an unfolded cube look like?" Kammie

The Renegade Success Plan

removed some tape from one of the cubes. "We could work backwards, you know, reverse engineer this cube."

Unfolded, the squares that made up the cube looked like a lowercase t. Four squares connected in a row, and two more were stuck to the sides of the second one in that row.

"Hmm, I wonder," Wren reached out and reattached one square in a different place.

She tried to refold it, but it didn't work. Wren flattened it again and stared at the pieces.

"I wonder how many ways you can arrange the squares so they'll still fold up into a cube?" Kammie pondered.

She began to assemble and reassemble some.

Applause came from Emma's table. Ivy looked over. Everyone looked excited. Ivy wondered what Axel's idea was. What was in those folders? She had a brief vision of

Caroline shaking Axel's hand, instead of her own. She shook her head to clear it and turned back to her own table.

Kammie, Amber, and Wren traced different patterns of squares onto sheets of cardstock.

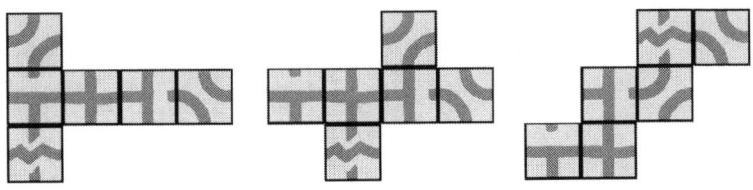

"We'll try out all these shapes to find one that folds easily into a cube and looks good." Amber cut out her shape. "When we get our prototype, my dad can put it in his graphic design software and print out some templates for us."

Amber folded a weird lightning bolt shape into a cube. Huh. It worked. These blocks really were interesting.

But would they interest an electrical engineer like Caroline? Not unless they included a robot that could play with the blocks. Caroline would never agree to be her mentor if they only had a few paper blocks to show her.

The image of Caroline shaking Axel's hand kept circling and circling in the back of her mind, as if it were on an endless path of its own.

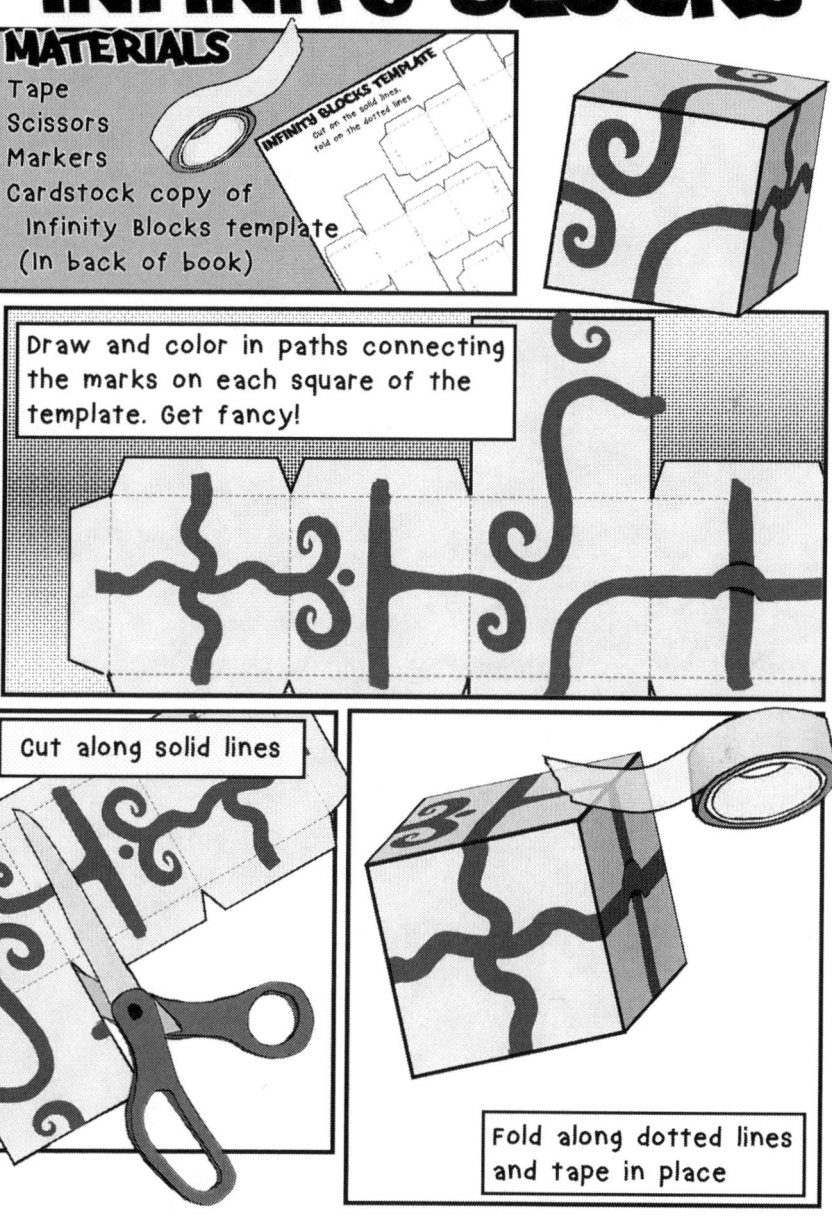

13

TECHNOLOGY!

"Who here is thinking of a future in technology?" Mrs. Mailloux asked in her French accent.

Social studies was Ivy's last class of the day. They'd spent most of the year learning about ancient civilizations, and, before the holiday break, moved on to modern topics like globalization, a fancy way to say that human societies were all connected, especially when it came to businesses.

Most modern countries couldn't really exist without each other these days. Just like how a computer and its components worked together, cities and countries relied on each other for the essential parts that come together to make whole products. Ships, planes, trucks, and trains moved stuff around, like wires sending electricity where it needed to go.

Ivy's hand shot up. "I'm going to be an electrical engineer."

"Okay, very good," the French woman nodded. "It's very impressive that you know so early what you will do. Let me ask you, what is technology?"

Ivy raised her eyebrows. How do you define technology?

"Technology," Ivy began, "is computers, electronics, you know. Robots and cell phones. Technology is the future. But see, everyone is going into software and coding. I want to build hardware. That's where the really exciting technology is."

Mrs. Mailloux nodded. "Indeed. When people think about technology today, they think of the electronics. But here is a question. Which of these is technology?"

She held up a pencil and a cell phone.

Ivy laughed. It had to be a joke, right? Mrs. Mailloux watched her expectantly.

"Umm. The phone is technology," Ivy replied. "The other is... a pencil. So, you know, not tech."

"BZZZZ," Mrs. Mailloux buzzed. "Incorrect! They are BOTH technology."

Ivy blinked. "I don't understand. How is a pencil technology? It's not a robotic pencil, is it?"

"We are surrounded by technology," Mrs. Mailloux set the pencil and phone back on her desk. "Class, this is common, to think that technology means electronic things. Actually, technology means inventions. Any kind of invention. Technology means using science, guided by engineering, to make things to solve problems. An engineer may create an invention to fix the problem they are trying to solve. That invention is called technology. Your pencil, the paper you write on, and even the languages we all speak are all inventions. They were created to solve the problem of remembering enough of what Mrs. Mailloux says to pass her test."

Everyone laughed.

Mrs. Mailloux wrestled a large, heavy box onto her desk. Various bits of electronics bulged out the top.

"Today, we are in the Fourth Industrial Revolution era. Everything is becoming digital. To explore our current technology, you will have a hands-on project."

She pulled raw circuit boards, a gigantic old cell phone, a printer with its outside cracked, even what looked like an old coffee maker out of the box. It was all e-waste—old, outdated electronics that weren't usable anymore, even though some had been cutting edge just a few years ago.

Next, Mrs. Mailloux pulled out a variety of screwdrivers, wrenches, and some little hammers. Then she brought out some small bowls.

"This is the sort of technology we use every day," Mrs. Mailloux began.

"Not THAT tech," scoffed Emma.

"*Mais non*," the teacher chuckled. "This is outdated, no? But it is not very old. And one issue our era has to deal with is what to do with this technology when we upgrade."

Across the room, Amber nodded vigorously. E-waste needed to be thrown away carefully. The electronic parts could leak dangerous chemicals into the ground.

"For our project, please choose groups and push your desks together."

Mrs. Mailloux handed screwdrivers and bowls to the kids as they shoved their desks together. Each group also got a bowl for screws and other little parts. Then she addressed the class.

"Your project today will be to look at these technologies from the inside. You will take them apart with these tools. Put the screws and small parts into your bowls. You use these devices all the time, it is important to be curious about how they are made."

The room got louder as kids called to each other and screwdrivers clattered onto desktops. Ivy wove through the shifting landscape of desks as their metal legs screeched on the linoleum floor. Amber pushed desks together with Emma and Tiffanie. Ivy joined them, accepting a screwdriver from the wandering teacher.

"Hey, Mrs. Mailloux," she glanced at the tool. "This is a flathead. Can I get a Phillips too? Most electronics use Phillips screws."

"You know your tools," the teacher looked through her screwdrivers and plucked another one out.

"This reminds me of when we took apart old clothes to see how they were made." Amber said to Ivy. "Maybe we can reassemble these parts into something new like we did with the clothes!"

Emma snagged the broken printer for them. She dumped it on the desk and grabbed a screwdriver.

"Hey," Emma looked at all the screws. "These don't match my screwdriver."

The tops of the screws on the printer all looked like little plusses. Emma's screwdriver looked like a minus. She tried it anyway but the flat end of the screwdriver was too big for the screw.

"Well that doesn't work!" Emma tossed down the screwdriver.

"You just need a different screw head," Ivy handed her the other screwdriver. The end of this one looked like a plus sign, too. "This type of screwdriver with a cross on the top is called a Phillips head. The other one is called a flathead. Most electronics use Phillips head screws."

"Who knew unscrewing things was so technical?" scoffed Emma, but she took the new screwdriver. "You know, I'm a little embarrassed to admit, I don't think I've ever really used one of these."

Amber blinked. "Really?"

"Yeah, I mean, what do I need to screw in?" Emma shrugged.

"Me neither," Tiffanie added. "It's kind of exciting. Let me try."

Tiffanie set the head of the screwdriver into a screw and turned it. The screwdriver turned but the screw didn't. The screwdriver popped out of the slots in the screw head.

"Did I turn it the wrong way or something?" Mused Tiffanie.

"Rightie tightie, leftie loosie. Turn it to the right to tighten a screw, and to the left to take it out, right Ivy?" Amber glanced at Ivy, then frowned. "Hey, pay attention."

Ivy shrugged. "Sorry, it's just that my mom's an electrical engineer. I've taken apart all kinds of electronics since I was a kid. You guys carry on."

"You could at least offer moral support." Emma poked her in the shoulder. "We're Team Printer!"

"Go team," Ivy said. "But speaking of teams, what's your team's project for the Expo? We saw you guys in the library. It looked interesting."

"It IS interesting," Emma glowed. "But I can't tell you. I've been sworn to secrecy."

Ivy perked up. "Ohhh, come on, you can tell me."

"Nope," Emma smiled. "Not gonna happen."

"Okay," Tiffanie bent over the printer, oblivious to the others. "Which way is right? I mean, I know which direction right is, but what does that mean when you're turning something? It goes in a circle. Everything is right at some point, right?"

"You go TOWARDS the left to take out a screw," Amber mimed twisting the screwdriver. "Imagine an old wall clock flat on its back. The direction its hands go is to the right. Clockwise is to the right. So counterclockwise, the reverse direction, is left."

Ivy continued to plead with Emma about her business. "Just give me a little hint."

Emma stuck her tongue out. "Dream on, lady. I know how to keep a secret. I can tell you our name though. We call ourselves Coderville."

Tiffanie twisted the screwdriver the correct way but it still popped out.

"This is stupid!" Tiffanie slammed the screwdriver onto the desk. "It doesn't work."

Ivy set the screwdriver's head into the screw. Pushing down first, she rotated the screwdriver to the left. The screw came out. More screws followed. They rattled together as she dropped them into the bowl.

"The trick to using a screwdriver," Ivy explained, "Is to push down with at least as much force as you turn with so your driver stays in the screw. It's helpful to get some leverage."

"Lever-what?" Tiffanie took the screwdriver back and tried again, gripping the tool as tight as she could. "That hurts my hand."

"Exactly," Ivy nodded. She motioned for Tiffanie to stand up and lean over the screw. "Leverage, in this case, means using gravity to your advantage. Get on top of it so you can kind of lean on it while you're turning. Then your arm doesn't have to provide all the pushing power to push down and turn at the same time."

Tiffanie tried it and finally got the screw out. She

dropped the little bit of metal triumphantly into the paper bowl with the others. "You're really smart, Ivy."

Ivy shrugged again. "Mom taught me a lot about taking things apart."

Emma unscrewed the last screw on the printer's cover. They took it off, revealing an intricate system of circuit boards, rollers, and gears. A box was mounted on a metal rod that spanned the width of the machine. A ribbon of multicolored wires connected the little box to the inside of the printer.

"What do you think that is?" Emma wondered out loud, tugging on the wire ribbon. The attached box slid along its rod. "Oh! It moves!"

"Maybe that's what pushed the paper through the printer," suggested Tiffanie.

Amber twisted a roller behind the box. "Or maybe this does. Which means the box slides sideways over the paper."

"I've got it!" Emma pointed to the box. "I bet that's the printhead! My printer always says 'Your printhead is jammed.' I bet it's that bad boy right there. Right Ivy?"

"I think so. Let's dig deeper."

The girls took apart the printer, piece by piece, trying to figure out what each part did. By the end of class, they had a bunch of small pieces in their bowl. And Ivy still hadn't managed to convince Emma and Tiffanie to tell her their business's secret.

"What do we do with these?" Emma asked, shaking the bowl full of screws and little pieces.

"That's the question," Amber frowned. "We make all this cool technology. We're constantly upgrading to the latest models, but what do we think is going to happen to our old ones? You can't throw electronics away in the trash. You have to recycle them in a special way."

Mrs. Mailloux nodded at Amber. "You are very right. There is a special box in the corner for all the larger electronic waste. I will bring that to the proper recycling place. And the art department wants to use these little pieces for their own project. So you may see them again. Thanks to the report you gave before winter break, I researched the right way to dispose of things."

"You were listening?" Amber asked.

"Yes, Amber, I was. If we can't use this technology any more for its purpose, I at least hope it has helped you be curious. We need people like you, *cherie*, to invent a better way to advance us to our next modern age."

A smile spread across Amber's face. She worked so hard to make a difference, to be the change she wanted to see in the world. It was nice to see it pay off. Ivy just hoped someday, maybe she'd be able to make a difference too.

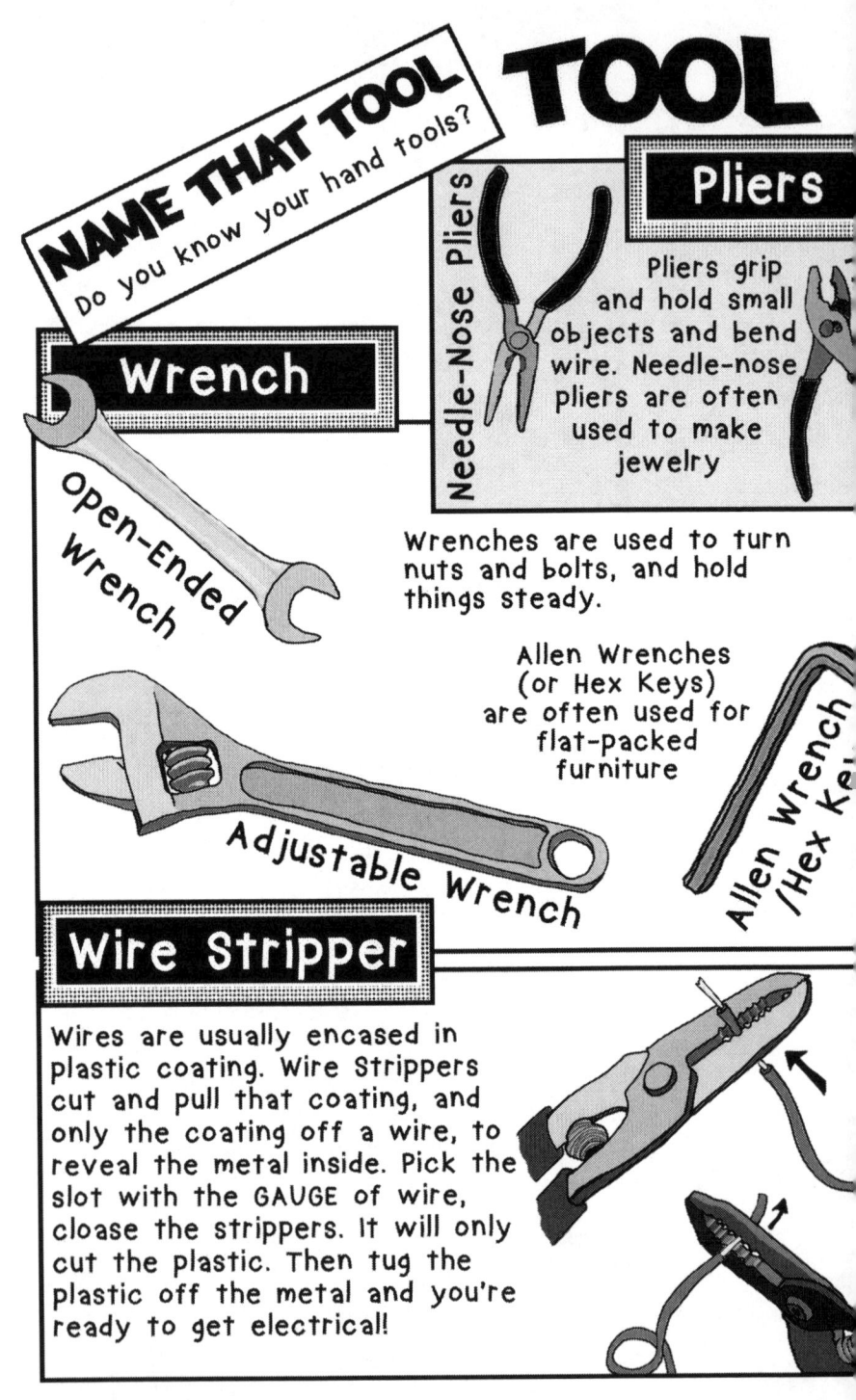

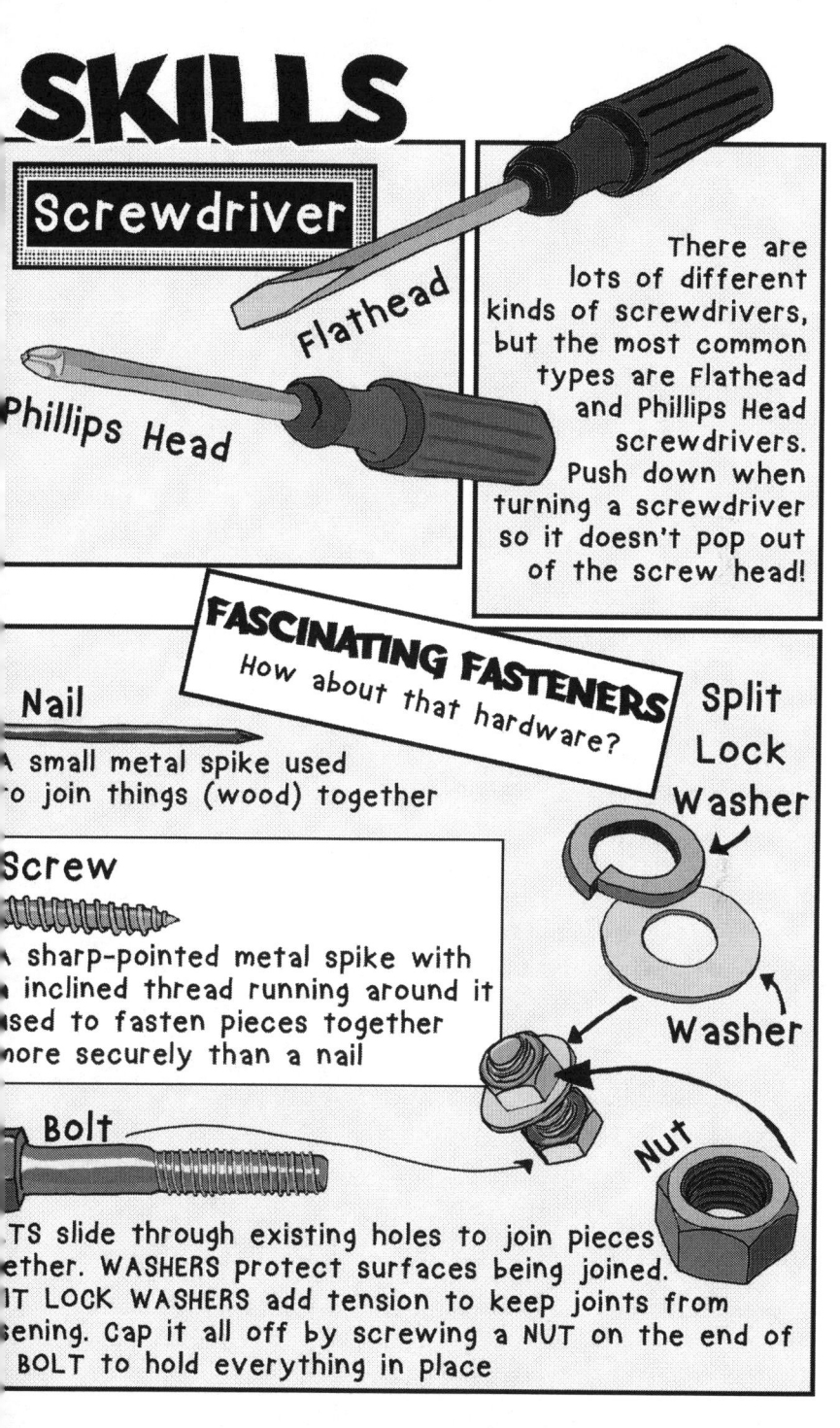

14

THE MYSTERIOUS BOX

Axel's team hovered around a large box that sat in the middle of their work table. A box Axel had carried through the library with a jacket over it. Emma and Tyrone discussed something in low, enthusiastic tones, but Ivy couldn't hear what they were saying.

The whole group clustered together as Axel opened its flaps. Ivy could hear gasps and happy noises as they peered inside the box. Axel carefully closed the flaps and slid the box underneath the table. She caught Ivy watching and put her finger against her smiling lips in a shhh sign before turning back to her group.

Meanwhile, at Ivy's table, Wren droned on about some upcoming school-wide quiz thing. It was for Career Week but had nothing to do with the Expo.

"I think it's on Monday the week before Career Week, so, I guess that makes it next Monday," she babbled. "Not like Monday next Monday but the next next Monday, right? We have two weeks before the Expo? I'm so excited! It's gonna tell me I should be a mechanical engineer, I just know it. Or a spy. Can a test tell you if you'd be a good spy? I bet it can, but what kind of questions would a test like that ask?"

No one was actually listening to her.

Kammie tested out color schemes with the Infinity Block cardstock templates Amber's dad had printed for them, coloring inside the lines with well programmed precision. Amber tinkered around with some trash. She had craft sticks, a straw or two, and some rubber bands. A bunch of leftovers she must have saved from the garbage.

Usually Ivy would be excited to build something out of random objects, but today the only thing that could excite her would be electronics. If she didn't find a way to introduce some modern tech into their toy company, then she was doomed for sure, and Wren didn't seem interested in expanding their product line. If only they'd decided to make a robot. Nothing would impress Caroline more than a robot.

Ivy's dream had returned last night. The one where she reached out to shake Caroline's hand, but instead the CEO had laughed and laughed at her.

Wren continued chattering. The quiz she was talking about was originally Kammie's group's idea from the brainstorm. Then it had grown in size and scope. Benjamin called it an aptitude test. Apparently, aptitude tests told people what sorts of jobs they'd be good at. The student council found someone to come in and administer one to the entire school. It was supposed to be fun.

Ivy didn't really see the point. What if you wanted to do something you weren't really that good at? With enough discipline you could be successful at anything you set your mind to. That's what her mom always said.

Maybe the test measured more than just your interests. Or maybe it would be as big a waste of time as listening to Wren talk about it.

Ivy angled her head around, trying to see the box under Axel's table without looking suspicious.

"What's IN there?" Ivy moaned. "What are they making?"

"What?" Wren broke off in the middle of a sentence. "I was talking, Ivy."

"Sorry," Ivy sighed. "But look, I don't really care about an aptitude test. Let's get on with the business stuff."

There was silence.

Shoot. Ivy must have missed something again. She really should pay better attention, but between trying to figure out what was in Axel's box, trying to figure out how to get REBELs Incorporated on track, and listening to Wren babble, sometimes she just couldn't keep track.

"What?" Ivy asked.

"Ummm," Kammie's soft voice was hard to hear over a bout of laughter from Axel's group. "Wren was already talking about business stuff."

"I was saying," Wren held up a piece of paper. "That we have to fill out this form to get a spot at the Expo. It talks about things like that gross and net profit stuff, something called revenue, and taxes. It's all super confusing."

"I can handle that," Ivy reached for the paper. Again, everyone looked at her. "What now?"

"Ummm," Kammie whispered. "I already volunteered to do that. But if you really want to, you know, it's okay."

"Oh," Ivy let her arm fall on the table. How long had she been wrapped up in her own world? "Sorry guys. I'm just concerned about getting us on track for the Expo. The blocks are great, but you can't build an entire company out of selling blocks."

"Tell that to LEGO," Wren snorted.

She had a point.

"We don't even know what our competition is doing," Ivy craned her neck around to look at Axel and Emma's group again. Then she noticed something strange.

All over the library kids were engaged in deep, animated discussions, even Bobby and Milo's group. No one was messing around anymore. They filled out forms, put together projects, and asked the librarian for research materials.

The librarian wasn't alone anymore, either. Coach Bakes wandered the tables, answering questions and, when needed, giving loud tables a firm look that brought the noise level down immediately. In fact, the whole library felt quiet and urgent as kids worked to make their companies great.

Every business in the whole school would be impressive except hers, Ivy realized. Everyone else looked like they were so much further along than REBELs Incorporated.

Ivy wished she knew what everyone else was doing. "I wonder if we're the only toy company."

"That's a good question. What do you think everyone else is doing?" Wren looked around the library, too.

Ivy chewed on her lower lip. "I wonder how we could find out?"

"Shouldn't we just worry about our own company?" Kammie asked.

"Good idea. You fill this out." Wren shoved the form at her, then turned back to Ivy and Amber. "Has anyone talked to any of the other teams?"

"Milo's group is doing something with sports," Amber offered. "I heard them talking about it. Or video games. Wait, I think their business is an esports league."

"Is that even a job?" Wren asked.

Amber shrugged. "I dunno. Playing video games professionally sounds more like a dream than a job. Seems like a weird idea."

"I bet Bobby's aptitude is being a criminal," Wren said with a spark of mischief in her voice. "He's got a great future in crime."

"Oh my gosh Wren!" Kammie looked up from the paper with a scandalized expression. "What a horrible thing to say."

"He'd probably never be caught anyway," Wren frowned. "He always gets away with everything."

"But," Ivy looked worried. "Do you think they've got a good business plan? I mean, is it better than ours?"

"It's not a competition Ivy," Kammie filled out the form. "It's supposed to be fun."

"You know what would be fun?" Wren nudged Ivy's shoulder. "Sneaking over and seeing what's in that box."

"Come on Wren," Kammie looked up. "We should just worry about growing our own business. You're the CEO, isn't that your job? Not get us in trouble?"

Wren blew a raspberry at her. "Remember? Trouble is just another word for adventure. Where's your sense of adventure?"

"If trouble is another word for adventure," Kammie mumbled, turning back to her writing, "then adventure is another word for trouble."

"I think knowing what the competition is doing is just good business," Amber whispered, leaning forward. "And there's nothing wrong with a little curiosity. Right?"

"Right!" A sparkle lit up Wren's eyes. She glanced at Axel's table. Then she took a deep breath. "But Kammie's right. We really should focus on REBELs. We should add another product to our lineup."

Ivy closed her eyes. She'd wanted nothing more than to brainstorm new, exciting products for their company. But now that Wren was finally ready to get it rolling, she couldn't even think about it. Her curiosity about the box enveloped her whole brain. The energy she visualized coursing through her body buzzed around her and pulled her towards that box like lightning to a lightning rod. She should be convincing the others that making a robot was a good idea. Now while there was still time. Whatever was in that box would get Caroline's attention a lot more than some pretty blocks. She should be creating an even better invention. But instead, all she could think about was the mystery of the box's contents.

Ivy had learned from her after school class that electricity started with atoms, the tiny building blocks that make up all matter. It took billions of atoms to make even the smallest object. Electricity was when one tiny part of an atom jumped from one atom to another, then another. Enough of those tiny parts, called electrons, all jumping in one direction created electricity, like drops of water moving in one direction to create a river.

And every drop of Ivy's energy river pointed towards that box.

Ivy was proud of Wren for fighting against her own curiosity, but of all the times Wren should control her impulses, well, this wasn't one of them. Right now, Ivy needed Wren's lighting.

And she knew just how to summon it.

"I dunno Wren," Ivy drawled. "Aren't you curious? What IS everyone else up to?"

"Leave her alone, Ivy," Kammie whimpered. "I can't get in trouble right now. Mom's still gone. She ran into some problems picking up my new brother. Dad's stressed enough as it is."

Ivy waved off her concern. Kammie's cautious nature usually kept them out of trouble but, again, now was not the time for it. If Ivy was going to have any hope of impressing Caroline, she needed to know what she was up against.

"Kammie's right," Wren said through gritted teeth. Her eyes kept darting to Axel's box and back. Her hands balled up into white-knuckled fists. "Let's stay focused. Shouldn't we? We should get back to business."

"Yes. We should." Kammie glowered at Ivy and Amber.

"Come on Wren," Amber smirked. "Don't you want to know what Axel's doing? I thought you liked being a field agent."

"After all," Ivy lowered her voice. "We ARE trained, card-carrying spies."

"Not REAL spy training," Kammie snipped. "Amber printed those cards out on her dad's computer."

"Details, details," Amber brushed the argument aside. "All that spy training, slowly rotting away."

"Cut it out," Kammie snarled. "We're not getting back into the spying business."

Wren looked up, her eyes sparkling. "Technically it's not SPYING. It's called corporate espionage..."

15

CORPORATE ESPIONAGE

They'd never get an opportunity like it again.

Most teachers let kids taking part in the Expo use a little class time to meet in the library and make up their classwork later. Usually there were dozens of kids packing the library tables.

Right now, there were only seven. And three of those seven were Ivy, Wren, and Amber.

They arrived just as Axel was about to leave. Ivy pretended not to watch her slip the box into her company's little storage cubby. The metal cubbies lurked in a back corner of the library, usually holding school deliveries or books the librarians were cycling in or out. They'd been temporarily cleared out for the Expo participants. Each company had one, and Axel's Coderville cubby got a lot of use.

"What are we going to do if she locks it?" Amber whispered as Axel wrestled the door closed with a click. "We didn't exactly study lock picking, you know."

"We'll just have to wing it. Who's left?" Ivy shrugged, pretending to discuss their business plan worksheet.

Wren looked around the room, pretending to stretch, "Emma, the baseball coach, the librarian, two boys from Milo's team, and another kid I don't know."

"Basketball," corrected Ivy.

"What?"

"You said baseball. Coach Bakes coaches basketball," Ivy clarified.

"Whatever," Wren rolled her eyes. "They both use balls and do a lot of running, don't they? They're practically the same thing."

Ivy didn't argue. It looked like most of the kids were on the far side of the library from the cubbies. Another stroke of luck. Only Emma was between them and the storage area.

Keep it simple. She just needed to move from their table to the lockers, get Axel's door open and check inside the box while no one was looking, close the door, and get back to the table.

Like a circuit, like her table was the battery and she was the electricity moving along a path, doing a job, then moving back again. As long as nothing got in her way, she'd be fine. Good thing Kammie wasn't here, though, with her resistors.

What they were doing wasn't really wrong, Ivy told herself. Nobody was going to get hurt, they weren't stealing anything, and everyone would know what was in that box soon enough. They were just getting a little sneak preview. A leg up on the competition. No big deal.

"Maybe I can get over there by bringing some stuff to our cubby," Ivy mused.

"You should check in Bobby's locker too," Wren suggested. "I bet he's up to no good. We'd be heroes if we busted him."

"Let's just focus on the one box for now," Ivy patted Wren's hands.

Wren pulled her hands away and frowned.

"What if someone sees you?" Amber asked. "We aren't supposed to be in the other cubbies. That's why they're letting us lock them."

"You'll just have to distract everyone, then." Ivy imagined herself at the lockers in the dark corner, putting their stuff away... looking around to make sure no one was watching... reaching over and sliding the door of another group's cubby open... reaching for the secrets inside...

BANG!

Strong adult hands smacked down on the table.

Everyone jumped.

"What are you doing?" Coach Bakes asked.

Ivy gasped. Wren and Amber exchanged terrified looks. How long had the coach been standing there? What had she overheard? They wilted silently under Coach Bakes' intense stare.

"Oh sorry," the coach laughed. "Didn't mean to scare you. I was just checking in."

Ivy breathed a sigh of relief. They hadn't been caught, she was just checking in. But with Coach Bakes around, the mission was a lot more risky.

Wren was the first to recover. "We're doing a toy company. Look! Infinity blocks!"

The coach eased herself into a seat and picked up one of the colorful paper cubes. She twisted it around and around.

"Neat," the coach smiled. "Have you considered packaging?"

Wren gave her a blank stare. "Huh?"

"You know," the coach leaned in. "how you package the product. I took a couple of courses in marketing when I was in college. Marketing is the stuff you have to do to sell a product."

A spark lit up Wren's eyes. Ivy could tell a lightning idea had struck.

"Oh! Fascinating," She smiled at the coach. "Do you think you could tell us about that? I saw something about that on the business plan form we have to fill out."

"Hmmm. I think I can do that," The coach sat up straighter. "I don't usually get the chance to talk about something not-sports related with you kids. Let's see those questions."

As the coach reached for the paper, Ivy nudged Wren's foot with her own. She understood Wren's idea, to distract the coach. But she wanted to silently tell her to invite the other kids over.

"Ow," Wren glared at Ivy. "Why are you kicking me under the table?"

Ivy tried hard not to facepalm. The coach looked up with a quizzical expression. Wren stared angrily at Ivy, waiting for an answer. Ivy thought fast.

"Sorry, I was just stretching." She'd just have to take matters into her own hands. "Hey, why don't we ask the other kids if they want to talk about it too?"

From her nearby table, Emma looked up. "What are you guys talking about?"

"Packing! Marketing!" Wren exclaimed, finally catching on, "All the -ings!"

Emma's face lit up. "I was just getting to that part of the business plan form thing. Does 'thing' count as an 'ing? I would love to talk it out together."

The other kids, overhearing them, also wanted to join in. It was working!

Emma and the other kids came over to their table, where Coach Bakes reviewed the questions on their form about marketing and packaging. Ivy stood.

Coach Bakes noticed immediately. "Where are you going, Park?"

"Umm, I wanted to get something out of our cubby."

Sitting next to the coach, Wren caught Ivy's attention and sent her a giant, overstated wink. Ivy tried not to roll her eyes. She just hoped the coach couldn't see Wren's face. Emma might have seen it though.

But Coach Bakes started talking. The kids actually seemed interested in what she was saying. Amber even took notes. Ivy grabbed the opportunity to head back to the cubbies and opened theirs.

Not much in there, just a few hand-colored blocks in different color schemes, one or two unfinished template printouts, and their tools. Scissors, markers, and tape. Nothing she could bring back to cover her tracks. She rifled through the stack of templates and saw the permit form they were supposed to turn in to get a spot in the Expo.

For a second, Ivy forgot about her spy mission completely. Weren't these supposed to be turned in already? By each company's CEO? Wren hadn't turned theirs in. Did that mean REBELs Incorporated wouldn't even get a spot? She knew Wren wasn't going to be the perfect CEO, but... this was serious.

Ivy pulled the form from their cubby and looked over at their table. Everyone else had their heads bent over whatever the coach was showing them except Wren. Who was watching Ivy. And waving!

Ivy motioned for her to pay attention to the lecture. Wren gave her a thumb's up over everyone's heads.

Oh my gosh, Ivy thought, anger flaring. *She's going to blow this whole plan.*

As soon as every head was looking at the paper the coach was filling out, Ivy reached over and tugged at the door to Axel's cubby.

It was locked.

Ivy's breath came faster. What could she do now? She looked around in desperation. Then a tiny metal object on the table between her group and the cubbies caught her eye.

It was a key.

The key to the cubby. Sitting on the table where Emma had left it.

But could Ivy get it and get back to the lockers without being seen? She'd just have to risk it. Her entire future was at stake. Eyes riveted on the group, Ivy edged over to the table. No one looked up. It was almost too easy. She grabbed the key in one fluid motion and zipped back to the shadowy corner where the lockers were.

Slipping the key into Axel's cubby, she turned it. The lock clicked. Ivy's eyes flitted towards the group. No one seemed to have heard.

She quietly opened the cubby door.

There, in the shadows, sat the mysterious box. Waiting. Ivy took one more look at the group. Amber was watching her. They locked eyes.

From the corner of her vision, Ivy saw Coach Bakes start to look up. If she saw her, Ivy was doomed. There was no explaining an open competitor's door, with a stolen key sticking out from the lock and her hands inside on something she shouldn't be touching.

Just for a moment, Ivy wondered if it was really a good idea, this corporate espionage. What would happen if she got caught? Was it worth it? And more importantly, was it the right thing to do? Sure, it didn't hurt anyone. These companies were just pretend after all. And it had been her idea. But was it really the right thing to do?

The Renegade Success Plan

Then she saw Amber attract the coach's attention with another question. Ivy felt a wave of gratitude wash over her for Amber's quick thinking. She needed to do what she came to do and get back to the table.

The box slid out from the cubby. Ivy looked down and read the writing on the side. Her stomach dropped.

It was a robot.

A robot from Dr. Kim's company.

Nothing could possibly impress Caroline more.

Ivy was doomed. Her entire future fell apart right in front of her, in a shadowy corner of her school library.

There would be no handshake. No seeing pride in her idol's eyes. No mentor opportunity. That would all go to Axel and Emma and their team. All Ivy had to offer were stupid colored blocks.

She stuffed the box back in and, distracted, slammed the locker shut loudly.

She looked around frantically and, at the same time, stepped away from the row of cubbies. The coach looked up and stared straight at her.

Maybe she wouldn't see which locker Ivy had slammed shut. Then again, did it really matter? What was the worst that could happen? Maybe she'd be thrown out of the Expo. That might actually be a blessing. But then, Ivy realized, it wasn't fair to the other Renegades. They were all working hard.

"Park!" The coach yelled.

Ivy braced herself.

"Get back over here. We're talking about some interesting stuff!"

Ivy almost fell down. The coach had no idea what she'd been doing. Ivy nodded and as soon as the coach looked down again, slipped Emma's key into her pocket on reflex and joined the crowded table.

She didn't even realize she still had the key until it was too late.

16

THE GAME

"I have no idea where I put that stupid key!" Emma complained to Ivy as she changed for the basketball game. "I mean, we have a few copies so it's not a big deal, but I hate losing things, you know?"

Ivy didn't say anything. It was early on Saturday morning. They were playing McKinley on their own court. It should be an easy win. But Ivy wasn't on form.

It wasn't just her unhappiness with the direction their company was going for the Expo. It wasn't just the fact that all her hopes and dreams were falling in a flaming heap at her feet and there was nothing she could do about it. It wasn't even the fact that she still felt uneasy about her own corporate espionage, even though it was over, no one was hurt, and it really didn't matter in the end anyway. It wasn't even how the key weighed in her pocket and she wasn't sure how to return it without giving herself away. It was everything put together.

Today, her mom was in the stands watching the game, but Kammie wasn't. Kammie and her dad were doing a video call with her mom, who was still in India trying to bring home her new brother. Ivy's mom had come to a game. Everything should be good. Better than good.

Ivy followed her teammates onto the court. When she closed her eyes and tried to see the buzzing white glow she was so used to visualizing around her body, it was barely there. Her battery was almost dead. Yes, that was it.

She felt dead inside.

And she played like she was dead inside. No hustle, no power. No electricity. After the first quarter, Coach Bakes pulled her aside.

"Park, you gotta look alive," she said. "Your team needs you."

"I know coach," Ivy agreed. "I'm on it. I'm just tired."

And she was. Tired in her body and soul.

Emma passed her the ball. She took it down court and sized up a shot. She summoned all her energy, visualizing it surrounding her arm. She took the shot, watching the trail of energy fizzle weakly between her hand and the ball. The trajectory was way off. She knew it wasn't going in from the moment it left her fingers. The white trail of its motion flickered, and went out.

A girl from McKinley recovered it on the rebound and drove it straight to her own basket. The shot gave McKinley the points they needed to pull ahead.

This was not the game Ivy would have chosen for her mom to come see. She had to turn it around.

At halftime, Coach Bakes looked her up and down.

"Okay Park," she said. "Something's going on with you. Take a break."

"But coach," Ivy protested. "The team is down. I have to get in there."

The coach shook her head. "You're no good to anyone like this, Park."

Ivy plopped on the bench with a heavy thunk. What kind of a success plan did she have now? She'd probably never even see her copy of Caroline Kim's book again. And what had she sacrificed it for? Wren probably hadn't even read it.

This is all Wren's fault, Ivy hated herself for thinking it, but the thoughts came anyway. *If she'd just let me be the leader, we'd be doing things differently. And I'd still have a chance to prove to Caroline that I'm the girl she saw in that stupid photo.*

Ivy twiddled her useless and empty fingers as the team played on without her. The referee blew her whistle. Ivy looked up. Emma had been fouled. She was on the ground. Maybe Ivy could sub for her.

One of the McKinley team helped Emma up and play resumed. The game went on and she remained on the bench. Ivy wanted to get out there and make a difference. But she was blocked everywhere. And there was nothing she could do about it.

She looked up just as McKinley scored again. She needed to get it together. Her team needed her. And her mom was watching from the stands. Ivy might not have power over what Wren did, or the direction their company was going, or how impressive Axel's business was. But she was here, in this gym, right now. There were plenty of things she could control.

"You're no one's victim," her mom always told her. "No matter what anyone else does, you always have options. You make your own choices."

There was a quote in *Success Plan*. Ivy wasn't sure who said it, but she remembered the words: *A dream written down with a date becomes a goal. A goal broken down into steps becomes a plan. A plan backed by action becomes reality.*

To get to reality, she needed a goal. Right here, right now. She wanted to win this game. She could start with that. That was her goal. This one game. She needed to get the ball in the net. To do that, she needed to be part of the team. She needed to pay attention to her arm position, to the power she shot through the ball, to how she flicked her wrist.

And then, she needed action.

"Coach Bakes," Ivy stood up and shook out her arms, glancing at her mother in the stands. "Put me in. I'm ready."

17

SILENT CODE THROWER

"So you won the game?" Kammie asked. "That's great."

Ivy dropped her gym bag near the door of the Greenhouse. She was even sweatier than usual, but flushed with success and ready to get stuff done.

Clouds covered the sky above Wren's backyard, but the day felt warm. She felt warm.

"It was close," Ivy explained. "But we pulled it out. I made the winning basket. I wish you could have been there."

"Congratulations," Wren looked up from something she was working on with Amber. "You're late though."

"Yeah, sorry. We kind of got wrapped up with celebrating. How's it going here?"

"It's okay," Wren replied. "Kammie was late too. Amber and I have been working on this."

"Everything okay?" Ivy asked Kammie.

"I guess so. Mom's stuck there for a while longer," She looked down at her hands. "I miss her."

Ivy put a hand on Kammie's shoulder.

Wren held up a mass of rubber bands and craft sticks, hot glued to a sheet of cardboard. She shook it, and the craft sticks rattled. Ivy couldn't figure out what it was supposed to be. Everything was stuck together in sort of a nest. Ivy tugged on a stick attached to a rubber band and let it spring back into place with a soft clatter.

"What's it supposed to be?" Ivy slid into her usual place across from Kammie.

"A way to communicate from across the room," Wren shrugged. "Like a walkie-talkie. We needed a better way to communicate with each other when you looked in Axel's cubby."

"It didn't really work out," Amber began to pull pieces off and toss them back into sorted piles.

Ivy froze and glanced at Kammie. The quiet girl across from her frowned at the rest of them. Wren must have told her all about their little reconnaissance mission. Ivy resisted the urge to groan. She hadn't planned on telling Kammie. Not really LIE to her. Just not mention it. She thought they had an unspoken agreement about not telling her, but apparently not.

"Amber told me you ran into problems when you did your spy thing," Kammie confirmed, disappointment and disapproval all over her face.

"So we're working on a code system?" Ivy tried to ignore Kammie's expression.

"Yeah," Amber replied, oblivious. "We need more products for the toy company anyway, right? What's more fun than secret messages?"

Ivy felt her shoulders relax a little. Finally! She probably wouldn't have picked walkie talkies to work on, but at least there was some action happening.

"So what's the problem?" Ivy asked, in true Engineering Design style.

"We need to communicate across a room, without anyone else knowing." Wren shook the mess of sticks and rubber bands. "This was supposed to be a sort of click code. Like, you pull certain areas and it would make certain sounds. Kind of like using different whistles to mean different things."

"But it needs to be secret, right?" Ivy mused. "So maybe sound-based codes won't work."

"What about something that disappears? Like disappearing ink," Kammie suggested. "Then you could read it from across the room and it wouldn't leave behind any evidence."

"But other people in the room could read it too," Amber pointed out.

"You're on the right track, though. Something visual." Ivy patted Kammie's back.

"OH!" Amber gasped. "What about color codes? Could we assign codes to particular colors and make colored cards or beads that we hold up?"

Wren nodded. "I can see that working. But you'd have to keep the colors simple. You couldn't really make out the difference between aqua and teal from across the room."

"Or even close up," Ivy added. "My color sense just isn't as good as yours. We could do stoplight colors. Red means stop, yellow means be careful, and green means go."

"That could work," Amber agreed. "How about a bracelet? It would be a pretty ugly bracelet, but you could turn it to each color and hold it over your head or something."

She grabbed a bin labeled 'LITTLE ROUND THINGS' and set it on the table. Inside were buttons, beads, weird Canadian coins, plastic rings, bottle caps, and other things harder to identify. Some had been organized into old mint tins, glass baby food jars, or baggies. Others had been thrown haphazardly in the bottom of the bin. Amber dug out a handful of large wooden beads in green, red, and yellow. She strung them on a bit of elastic cord and slipped it over her wrist.

"Now, if I..." She turned it so the red beads were at her wrist and lifted her hand above her head.

"That's yellow," said Wren.

"Wait, no," Ivy corrected. "Mostly red. But a few green"

"I guess it depends on where you're standing. Since Wren is on this side, she sees one part, and you see a different part on the other side," Amber dropped her hand. "Besides, it's not very stylish. It would look suspicious if I wore something so ugly."

The Renegade Success Plan

"And if Ivy wore a bracelet at all!" Kammie pointed out.

Amber, Kammie, and Wren took the bracelet apart, talking about ideas to use more attractive beads, or beads you could rearrange to make color coded messages.

Ivy barely listened to them.

She was getting bored. Beads, bracelets, blocks. None of them were impressive. How could she get at least a simple circuit in there? What if the color could spin or glow or something?

She thought back to the purse they'd invented and it's three glowing flowers. Could they do something like that? The flowers had been pulled from discarded clothing, and their circuit had been sewn directly into the purse's fabric. Ivy had used metal magnetic snaps on the flap so when the metal snapped together, it completed the circuit and lit up the lights.

But it didn't have to be magnets. Or even sewn. In a spy gadget they'd invented, they straddled the legs of an LED light around a coin cell battery. Then they'd used cardboard to hold the battery in place and keep the legs from touching both sides of the battery at once so the light was off. All they had to do was squeeze the legs a little so they both touched the battery at the same time and the light lit up.

The concept was the same both ways. When you wanted a light to light up, you had to create an unbroken path for electricity to move from one side of the power source to the light, then back to the other side of the power source. If you broke that path anywhere along the circle, the electricity stopped and the light went out. That was the idea behind a switch, whether the switch was on the wall of a room or was a metal snap, the idea was the same.

"What if we use light?" Ivy mused out loud.

"Light?" Amber thought about it. "Like an LED?"

"What does that have to do with beads?" Wren asked.

"Nothing," Ivy replied. "Not beads at all. Different direction. What if we do a flashlight? One that you squeeze to turn on and let go to turn off?"

"OH!" Kammie perked up. "Like Morse Code? Dot dash dot dot and stuff? I read about that in one of my code books."

"A Silent Code Thrower!" Wren announced. "That would be fun."

Ivy looked for something she could hold in her hand. Something long and thin. She picked up a discarded craft stick.

"When I accidentally made that catapult," Wren squinched her mouth in thought. "I used two craft sticks rubber banded together with some paper wedged between them. One end of the sticks stayed together, and the other end didn't touch. I bet if you used less paper, or a spring instead of paper, the ends would touch when you squeezed it, and only when you squeezed it. That's what you want, right?"

"Yup!" Ivy took a second craft stick and rubber banded it to the first.

Wren started digging in a random bin while Ivy got out

an LED, a coin cell battery, and some short bits of wire with the plastic stripped off the ends.

"What's the wire for?" Amber asked.

"The leads of the LED aren't very long," Ivy showed her the small metal legs coming down from the LED's bulb. "So we need to make them longer. Metal is conductive, which means electricity moves through it easily. So, wire!"

"We could use tin foil," Kammie suggested.

"Yeah, that might work too, but wire is made for the job, and plus, we have some." Ivy wrapped one end of each wire around one of the LED's leads, then bent them in half.

Amber handed her some stretchy electrical tape and she wrapped that around the wire and bent LED lead. Then Ivy undid the rubber band and taped one leg of the LED and its wire to each craft stick. Now all they needed was a battery.

"Found one!" Wren held up a spring. "This sucker was hiding. I think it's from a pen or something."

Ivy hesitated. "That won't work. It's tall and skinny. And metal, which is a conductor. We need something smaller. Just big enough to hold them apart."

Wren's smile faded.

"I thought we said we'd use one of these," Wren dropped the spring back into the bin with a frown. "So, what are we going to use then?"

"I liked your idea of paper, actually," Ivy replied,

trying to soothe her. "Paper is an insulator, not a conductor. It stops electricity."

"I'm always amazed by how much you know about this stuff," Kammie said quietly. "It's super confusing to me and you keep saying all these new words."

Ivy smiled at her. "I'm not going to test you. It's just something I've been learning for a really long time. That's all. Like how you speak those other languages. I mean, I understand a little Korean from my grandparents but I never learned to speak it myself."

"I'm still impressed," Kammie blushed. "Oh, speaking of ideas, I kind of had a little one. Do you guys want to hear?"

Kammie dug into her bag and pulled out a tiny cardboard box. Something rolled around inside. She also pulled out a few slightly squashed infinity blocks.

"Look!" She held them close to each other, and they snapped together.

Wren dropped her bin.

"Whoa! That's cool! Magnets?"

Kammie nodded. Inside her little box was a stack of tiny round magnets. "Dad says you have to keep small magnets away from babies or they might eat them. So, he told me to bring these here."

Ivy used the electrical tape to finish securing her LED. Then she folded a bit of paper and taped it between the leads. A "silent code thrower", Ivy thought to herself with a grin. While she finished it up, the others taped magnets on the inside of each face of a few infinity cubes.

The last step on the code thrower was to add the battery to one side, making sure to cover as little of the battery's surface as possible.

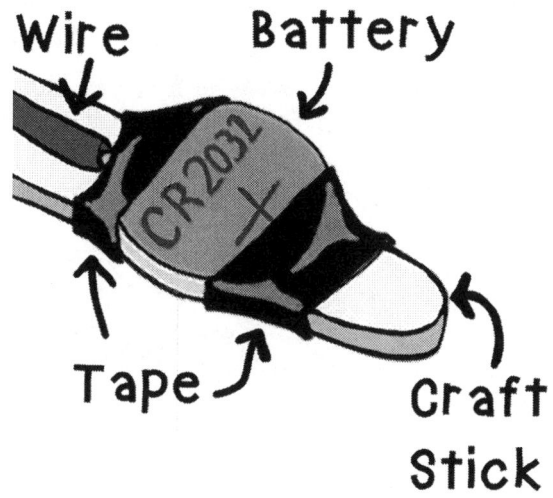

That was it. It seemed complicated, but was surprisingly simple. She squeezed it.

The light didn't light up.

Over on the table, Amber was having the same kind of problem. Her blocks wouldn't snap together. Once she got them close to each other, they'd fight back and spin around, snapping to a different side.

"Weird," Amber mused. "But fun."

"Yeah," Wren agreed. "It's almost like a puzzle now."

"A puzzle that can stick to a refrigerator!" Kammie grinned.

Ivy flipped her battery around, tested her code thrower

again, and the light lit up. She held it up for the others to see. "It works!"

"Great!" Wren said. "We're really moving now!"

Ivy had to agree. They might have originally made the code thrower to do a little corporate espionage, but it could be a toy too. And it was electronics! Nothing that would impress Caroline, but a step in the right direction.

With the new addition to the infinity blocks, though, maybe they were at least getting there.

Maybe.

SILENT CODE THROWER

MATERIALS
- 1 LED
- 1 rubber band
- 2 craft sticks
- 1 small piece of paper
- electrical tape
- 1 coin cell battery
- 2 insulated wires about 3 inches long with ends stripped

Wrap raw end of wire around the LED's leads and bend. Wrap each in electrical tape, covering leads

Tape battery on one stick and the raw ends of the other wire on the other stick

Straddle an LED on the tip of a craft stick. Tape top wire down and wrap raw end to underside

They should touch when squeezed

Fold up some paper and insert between the two craft sticks

Wrap a loose rubber band around the sticks.

Squeeze to light it!

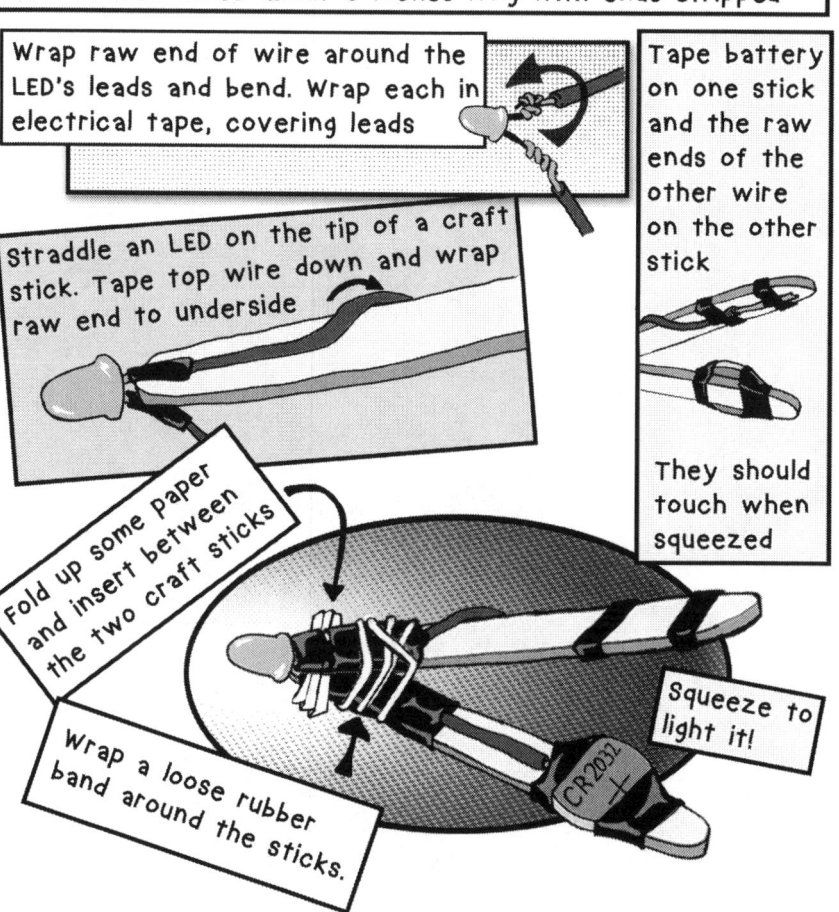

18

STATISTICS

Monday hit like a hammer. Next week was Career Week, so they only had ten school days and one more weekend until the Expo. And, since it was Career Week, next week would be busy with lots of guest speakers and special classroom activities. Meanwhile, the Lovelace Machines were doing great. With each win, basketball practice intensified. Each win put them up against better teams. Each new success led to the pressure to keep succeeding. But the Expo loomed like a heavy dark storm cloud. Every time Ivy thought about it, she started breathing heavily. Caroline was coming, and she wasn't ready.

When she closed her eyes, instead of strong electricity flowing through her or even the dead-battery faded glow of exhaustion, Ivy saw a hot circuit ready to explode. Sparks buzzed and leapt out. She'd even yelled at her mom this morning. That hadn't gone well.

But they were getting somewhere.

"Hey Wren, did you turn in that form for the Expo?" Ivy asked. "The one I found in our cubby?"

"Oh, oops," Wren replied. "I was just going to do that today."

Ivy groaned. "Can you please take care of that?"

"I know, I know," Wren waved Ivy's concern away. "I'm on it. There's just so much to take care of. Our spy business wasn't this hard. There's permits and applications, and business plans and revenue and taxes and blahdy-blah blah. I thought this Expo thing was going to be easier than going to class!"

"At least we're learning how hard it is to start a business for real," Kammie pointed out.

That realization didn't seem to make Wren feel any better.

Amber pulled out a stack of printed cardstock and flopped it on the library table. Next to them, a few boys from Milo and Bobby's team looked over.

"What's that supposed to be?" One of them asked with a sneer.

"None of your business," Wren answered.

"Whoa, settle down," he chided. "Don't get all emotional."

Wren glared at him. "I will get exactly as emotional as I want to get. I've seen you guys freaking out over your stupid esports. Don't call me emotional when you stomp around and throw pencils because your little video warrior got shot."

Milo snorted out a laugh. The boy turned back to his own table.

The final printouts of the Infinity Blocks looked good. Each of six different pathway patterns was printed three times, one in each of the three color schemes Amber chose. She'd colored them in with her Dad's software, not markers, so they looked less homemade. When they were cut out and folded up, they'd have three sets of six, or, eighteen blocks. Ivy had to admit, she really liked them.

They needed a lot of Kammie's magnets. Each block needed one on each of its six sides, and there were lots of blocks. That equaled a lot of magnets. One hundred and forty-four magnets to be exact. Even though they were reusing the original ones, Kammie's dad had needed to order even more online.

"We'll tape these magnets exactly in the center of each block so they'll match up with each other." Kammie pulled out a ruler. "The easiest way to find the center of each side is to draw lines diagonally from corner to corner. The middle of the X is the middle of the side. Tape the magnet right in the center of the X."

Wren started cutting out a block. "How did you guys do on the aptitude test this morning? I bet I got an A!"

They'd taken the test in the morning. It had been harder than Ivy thought it would be. A bunch of questions didn't even make sense. How could a lot of random questions find out what jobs or skills you'd be naturally good at —your "aptitude"? It was a bunch of trouble for nothing, in her opinion. What test could predict what a kindergartener was going to be when they grew up?

But Benjamin, and everyone else, thought it would be fun. Ivy seemed to be the only one who didn't think it was very practical. The results weren't going to make any difference to anyone. Their time was better spent on their REBEL business.

"Let's talk about expanding our product line." Ivy started cutting out a printout.

"I've got this," Wren scowled. "I'm the CEO. You seem to forget that an awful lot."

Ivy bit her lip.

"She's just trying to help, Wren," Amber offered.

"I don't need help," Wren continued to scowl. "Nothing's broken."

"Your idea is dumb." The boy from Bobby's table tilted his chair onto it's back two legs and hung his head over the back, looking at them upside down. "Toys are for babies."

"You're a baby," Wren snipped, brandishing the scissors at him. "Don't make me spank you."

"Yikes!" The boy threw his hands up in pretend fright, almost tipping over backwards. He quickly dropped his chair forward onto all four legs again with a real squeak of fear.

"Don't worry Albert," Bobby said loudly. "Our idea is going to beat theirs. Then we'll see who's crying like a baby."

Coach Bakes looked over at them. Ivy felt her blood

rising with anger, but in the back of her mind she was scared they might be right.

"Nobody's going to beat anyone," Amber replied calmly. "It's not even a competition."

"Competition or not," Bobby sneered. "we're not going to be beat by a bunch of girls!"

Milo froze, looking at Bobby angrily. Before he could say anything, Wren turned on Bobby with fiery eyes.

"What, exactly, is that supposed to mean?" Wren growled.

"It's just statistics," Bobby shrugged. "Men do better in business than women. Look at the number of man CEOs in big businesses and the number of girl CEOs. It's just math."

"Because men have more OPPORTUNITY," Wren snorted. "Your precious statistics are wrong. We are gonna wipe the floor with you guys. And it's not even a competition. BAM, you're gonna get businessed!"

A proud smile crept over Milo's face as he gazed at Wren's blazing expression. He elbowed Bobby. "Yeah, man. BAM."

"Actually, it's not just the opportunity." Bobby leaned closer. "Statistics show that boys have stronger spatial skills, are more assertive, and do better in math and science."

"Don't mansplain me, Bobby Butthead," Wren grabbed around the table randomly, her hand falling on a wad of paper. She hoisted it up and looked at Ivy. "Can I throw this at him?"

"First off, boys don't do better in math and science than girls. That's a myth." Kammie's soft voice caught their attention. "And secondly, that's not how statistics work."

Bobby rolled his eyes. "You can't argue with math, Kammie."

"No, you're right," Kammie looked straight at Bobby. "That's why you're wrong. Statistics work in aggregate. That means they work for large groups of people. Not individuals."

Bobby paused. "What does that mean?"

"A group of people might be higher than another group in some way on average, but that doesn't mean anything to any pair of given points of data."

"You're just saying a bunch of words," Bobby replied. "You're trying to confuse me."

"That's not hard," Wren scoffed.

Milo laughed, then choked to a stop when Bobby turned to glare at him.

"What dude," Milo shrugged. "That was funny."

Milo glanced again at Wren and smiled mischievously.

"Say that again in English." Bobby looked less sure of himself.

"I mean," Kammie's voice got a little louder, "that the statistics of a whole group don't necessarily apply to the individuals in the group. Like, even if boys as a group are, say, better at shooting a basketball than girls as a group, that doesn't mean you, Bobby, can make more baskets than Ivy."

Ivy smirked at Bobby. He looked away.

"BAM!" Wren cried. "Forget business, you just got MATHED!"

"I'll still have an easier time getting a job than you," Bobby sneered at Wren.

"Hey, that's not cool." Milo smacked him upside the head. "I wouldn't hire you, you big dummy."

Coach Bakes stood up, looking at their tables.

The boys turned back to their own table and the Renegades turned back to theirs. Wren seethed quietly.

"Um," Amber tried to change the subject. "I'm going to think of another product for us."

"Why not," Wren grabbed her backpack. "Apparently no one has any faith that I can make a good company."

"That's not what I mean," Amber said.

Wren stomped out of the library. Ivy watched her go, unsure what to do. She had her own doubts about the direction of their company, but nobody was allowed to hurt one of her best friends.

Ivy's hand slid into her pocket. The smooth craft sticks of their Silent Code Thrower slipped into her palm. There was no basketball practice today. She could stay a little late. She might never actually use the Code Thrower to send signals, but it would make a perfect flashlight for once the sun started going down. Maybe a little more corporate espionage could set things right.

If Bobby and his crew were so sure of themselves, it wouldn't hurt to get a little peek at what they were doing.

19
SOLO MISSION

It wasn't wrong, Ivy told herself. It's not cheating. She'd just take a look at Bobby's team's progress. It wouldn't hurt anyone, they'd never even know. Besides, they deserved it.

School was over for the day, and almost no one was left in the library. No one from Bobby's group, no one from Axel's, none of the other Renegades, not even the librarian. Only a few scattered kids and Coach Bakes, who had her feet kicked up on the librarian's desk, reading a book.

Perfect.

She really didn't want the others there anyway. Kammie didn't approve of spying, and Wren was terrible at it. Amber might be a good spy, but she wasn't good at keeping secrets from the rest of them. Besides, for them it was just a game. No one else cared that Caroline would be at the Expo, that she'd be looking for the innovators of tomorrow. No one else understood how important it was to stand out.

It was up to Ivy.

She looked around the silent library. The door creaked open to admit two eighth graders Ivy didn't know. They waved to Coach Bakes and sat at another table. That made... Ivy counted... four kids and the coach, not counting herself.

Still perfect.

If she'd been alone with the coach, she'd never be able to sneak over to the cubbies and dig around.

She flopped her bag on top of the table closest to the cubbies' dark alcove and pulled out a notebook, the business plan, the code thrower, and her unfinished math homework. Might as well take care of that while she was here.

Ivy settled in to wait for the right opportunity to infiltrate the cubbies and start spying. While waiting, she finally looked over the REBELs business plan form. Executive summary, company summary, market analysis, management team, and revenue projections. Pretty dry stuff, she couldn't imagine Wren actually staying focused long enough to answer the questions. Kammie had filled in some answers, but Ivy didn't bother reading it. She wasn't in charge, after all. Setting it aside, she finished off a few questions on her math homework.

The noise level in the library rose as kids discussed their own business plans or how to set up their booths for the Expo. Hopefully Wren had turned in the form for their Expo table.

Coach Bakes stood up and Ivy pulled the business form in front of her so it looked like she was reviewing it. But the coach passed by her to answer some questions for the eighth graders.

It was the opportunity Ivy was waiting for.

Ivy grabbed the code thrower. They probably wouldn't ever actually use it to send codes, but it made the perfect spy flashlight. She slipped into the dark alcove, squeezing the sticks together. The LED's tiny light lit up a small circle on the doors of the cubbies, and nothing else. No one would see it from out in the library.

Next problem; which cubby belonged to Bobby? There were about twenty of them. Ivy shrugged and tugged on the closest door.

It was locked.

She tugged harder. The door rattled. Ivy froze, eyes darting to the coach, but no one had heard it. The next door was locked too. Darn it. Ivy hadn't expected everyone to lock their secrets away.

Door after door resisted her tug until, finally, one opened. A bunch of papers lay haphazardly inside. Ivy pulled out the top one and brought the light of the code thrower closer.

A shoe store, selling high-end sneakers. Ivy rolled her eyes. At least their toy company was better than that. She closed the door and moved on.

Three more locked and two unlocked doors later, Ivy

finally found the one she was looking for. And they hadn't locked the door.

The cubby only contained paper, so it made sense they hadn't locked it. They had a lot of kids on their team and only a few keys. They weren't making any products and didn't have to store anything valuable like a robot, so leaving their cubby door open made sense. Luckily for Ivy.

She got to work, pulling out the papers and reading them as quickly as she could. They hadn't turned in their Expo form either, and then she saw why. Under "Management Team," they'd listed eight names. All with the title president.

That was no way to run a company. Someone had to make decisions. Otherwise, how would you get anything done, and who would take responsibility? Too many cooks spoil the soup, they said.

What about Axel's team? How were they structured? Since she was here anyway, maybe she could just take a little look. Who would know?

She'd never found a way to get the key to Axel's cubby back to Emma. It was in the front pocket of her backpack on the table. She could just slip out, grab it, and slip back. She pushed the papers back into Bobby's cubby and quietly closed the door.

She turned to sneak back to the table. And froze.

Coach Bakes stood before her, hands on her hips.

"That doesn't look like your storage locker, Park."

Ivy's mind raced. When had the coach noticed her? What had she seen?

The Renegade Success Plan

"I... I... Um," she stuttered. "I mean, I was just..."

The coach crossed her arm across her chest and raised her eyebrows. Ivy writhed under her gaze then gave up trying to explain herself. She hung her head.

"I'm sorry. Their door was unlocked. I just wanted a peek."

"Your friend Axel Andrews just wanted a peek at the election results at the beginning of the year," the coach said in clipped tones. "You might remember how much trouble that caused the entire school."

Ivy's head shot up. Her spying was nothing like Axel stealing the election results. It was totally different. At least it FELT totally different. But maybe that's because she was on the other side of it this time. Maybe it wasn't so different after all. Was it?

"I'm disappointed in you, Park," the coach shook her head. "I expected better of you."

"Everyone always does," Ivy sighed. "I won't do it again. I promise. I didn't even see anything."

Coach Bakes tapped her foot. The silence stretched on. Then, the coach sighed.

"Alright," she waggled her finger in Ivy's face. "But don't let me catch you 'not seeing anything' again. I expect my team to play fair."

The coach walked back to the librarian's desk. Ivy let out a huge breath, leaned back against the cubbies, and slid to the floor. That was close.

Next time, she'd have to be more careful.

20

SPLINTERED

Ivy carried her lunchbox towards the recess yard. The Renegades would be waiting for her at their usual picnic table. She'd have to be careful what she said to them. Watch her words carefully. Ivy didn't like secrets, but she couldn't tell them about last night.

Winter sun shone down on kids bouncing off each other and the playground equipment. Yelling to each other, throwing balls. Disorderly. Chaotic.

Splintered.

Wren sat on top of the picnic table, ripping off bits of her bagel and stuffing them into her mouth. Cream cheese smeared on her fingers and around her mouth. She was in static electricity mode, Ivy noticed. Zappy and annoying. Wren's big, messy smile, so full of unfiltered energy, didn't bring her joy today. How could someone who couldn't even eat a bagel without making a disgusting mess all over their face, possibly lead her team to victory?

The Renegade Success Plan

As she wove through some kids playing basketball, Ivy noticed Axel's perky blonde ponytail. Axel rarely ate outdoors, but today she sat with Emma and all the rest of the kids from her group. She was smiling and eating a bagel too, but didn't have cream cheese smeared everywhere. She and all the other kids of their Coderville business huddled together over someone's iPad.

They seemed excited, involved. Successful. A winning team.

Ivy wondered if she could switch groups. It wouldn't mean she was abandoning her friends. Would it? No, the Renegades were her team, and you didn't just abandon your team because they were on a losing streak. You fought to help them win.

Her steps slowed as she watched Coderville's excitement. She still stared at them as she sat down. Wren's voice babbled on, sounding far away.

"Why do you think they're doing a second aptitude test?" Wren wiped her mouth. "And why the heck is it on a weekend?"

Amber and Kammie stopped eating.

"What do you mean?" Amber asked.

"The other test." Wren grabbed her water bottle. "Trixie and I are supposed to go in for ours on Saturday. So, I'll miss our club meeting. Which is dumb, but mom insisted. When are you guys going in?"

The others looked at each other.

"Nobody said anything about a second test," Kammie answered. "Did I miss something?"

Amber shook her head. "I didn't hear anything about it either. How about you Ivy?"

"Nope," Ivy chewed on her ham sandwich. "The first one wasted enough time."

Wren blew a raspberry at her. "Where's your sense of adventure? It's FUN. There doesn't have to be some big boring purpose to everything. Geeze."

Ivy glanced over at Axel's group again. They were heading in, probably to the library to work on their robot stuff. Now THAT would be fun. Ivy sighed.

"Hey Wren," she tried to sound casual. "Did you like *Success Plan*?"

"I... ummm... you mean that book you lent me?" Wren coughed.

"Yes," Ivy nodded. "Don't tell me you haven't read it yet."

Wren's eyes darted around. "Umm. I'm not done with it yet."

Ivy would never see the book again. Wren would never read it. It was probably lost in her mess of a room.

A shadow passed over her sandwich. She looked up. Axel smiled at them. Ivy looked into Axel's blue eyes and suddenly felt a strange connection with her.

"Hi guys," Axel said pleasantly. "How's your business going?"

"Fine," Wren replied with a cold tone. "Why do you care?"

To Ivy's surprise, Axel just smiled. "I'm glad. I just wanted to let you know we're going to announce part of our business today in the library. In case, you know, you were interested."

"Why?" Wren seemed like she expected a fight, or some of Axel's usual snark. But the blond girl just laughed.

"If you're not interested, that's fine," Axel shrugged. "We're telling everyone and I wanted to make sure you guys knew. I think you'll like it. Okay, bye."

Then she turned with a flip of her ponytail and pranced back into the school.

Ivy stuffed the rest of her lunch into her lunchbox without even eating her chips. "Come on, guys, let's go see."

Amber stood to follow Ivy, but Wren didn't budge. Ivy rolled her eyes with an impatient sigh. Wren didn't have to join them, she could pout out here all she wanted. But Ivy was going. She headed towards the library without checking to see who else joined her.

THE ROBOT'S sleek white metal body and black rubbery joints almost glittered in the sun. Two bright blue eyes, probably sensors, perched at the top of its head. It stood about two feet tall, battling against gravity to stay upright on two legs and taking cautious robotic steps across the library table.

It walked three paces, wobbled to a stop, and settled its body down to the tabletop. Once the body was down, the legs folded over and became wheels.

Then the robot drove in a circle.

The library erupted in applause. Axel and Emma high-fived while Tyrone hugged one of the other kids in the group. There were at least a dozen other kids watching and all of them congratulated Axel's team. She smiled and thanked them all, patting the robot on its head.

Ivy squinched her mouth up into a ball. It was the third successful demonstration, and Ivy just couldn't watch it anymore. She was too jealous. She sat at her own table and folded a paper block.

"Hey, do you think it's Arduino based?" Kammie asked, watching the robot with wide eyes. "I've never programmed an Arduino board. Do you think they'd let me try?"

"The company is all about the code," Ivy snapped. "Not the robot. It's just a toy they bought from Sapai, Dr. Kim's company. If you wrote code for them, you'd be on their team. And you're not."

Kammie blinked and turned to stare at Ivy.

"Gosh, I'm sorry," she said. "I was just wondering."

Ivy's expression softened. "I'm sorry Kam. I'm not mad at you. I'm just having a bad day."

She didn't admit that she wanted to be on their team too.

"Maybe they'll mess up," Wren, who'd come to see after all, narrowed her eyes at the robot. "Get a bug in their code."

"Did you know that expression came from an actual bug inside a computer?" Kammie giggled.

"No way, really?" asked Wren.

Ivy didn't listen to them as they droned on. She wanted to leave. Why had she even come here in the first place? To watch a super impressive robot steal everyone's attention the way it was going to steal her future?

"Yeah, Grace Hopper was this early programmer," Kammie continued on the other side of the table. "She developed the very first programming language that used regular English words instead of math to talk to computers. Without her, it would be a whole lot harder to write code! Back then, computers were really big and had all these moving parts. One day her computer wasn't working right, and she found an actual MOTH inside it!"

"That's hilarious!" Wren laughed.

Another round of applause came from Axel's table.

Ivy couldn't take it anymore. She stood up and grabbed her bag.

"Hey," Amber called. "Where are you going?"

Ivy didn't even answer her. She just walked out, feeling terrible but unable to stop her feet from carrying her away.

21

ANTS

A tiny black ant crawled along Amber's snow-white countertops. It was Saturday, and Wren and Trixie were off doing their extra testing. The Renegades didn't feel right meeting in the Greenhouse without Wren, so they all gathered in Amber's kitchen instead.

Without Wren, though, they weren't getting much done. Ivy rested her head on her folded arms on the counter. An ant crawled towards some orange juice Amber's little brother had spilled.

Amber's mom crushed the ant with a paper towel.

"MOM!" squealed Amber. "What did you do?!"

"Oh please, honey," her mom tossed the towel and ant into the compost bin. "Let's not start."

"It's MURDER Mom!"

"It's an ant, Amber, for goodness sake."

"Ants are amazing! Did you know ants are one of the strongest animals for their size? Or that they can be found on every continent except for Antarctica? Ants have an important role in our ecosystem."

"Well they DON'T have an important role in my kitchen," her mom sounded exasperated, but Amber kept going.

"We have to learn to coexist with nature," Amber insisted. "If we're going to continue to live on this planet."

"Nature is not allowed to coexist in my kitchen," her mom tore another paper towel off the roll. "And that's final."

With one swipe, Amber's mom cleaned up the spilled orange juice and another few ants with it. She slid everything into the compost bin. Then she patted Amber on the head and walked out of the room.

Amber watched her go with a mix of anger and resignation. When she turned back to Ivy, her eyes brimmed with tears.

"It's so sad," Amber sniffed. "That poor little ant. She finally finds an abundant food source for her colony, only to be thrown into the compost with it. To become food herself."

"Don't you mean he?" Ivy asked. "It was just a regular ant, not a queen."

"Oh no, it's not like all ants are boys except for the queen. The queen is just the only one who can lay eggs," Amber wiped away the tears and glanced at the compost bin. "That's the circle of life, I guess. When I die, I hope they leave my body on the Serengeti to get eaten by lions the way nature intended."

Ivy cringed.

Kammie changed the subject. "I wonder how Wren is doing. What do you think the test is for?"

"Mom probably knows," Amber pouted. "But she's not telling me anything."

"I hope she's okay," Kammie whispered.

"It's probably to see why she's so annoying," Ivy tried to joke, but the comment came out more bitter than she'd intended.

Amber tilted her head at Ivy. "Annoying, huh? She's being a lot less annoying than you lately. You've been so grumpy. What's wrong?"

That caught Ivy by surprise. She'd assumed everyone else was tired of Wren messing up like she was. The idea that SHE was the one being annoying had never occurred to her. Could Amber be right?

"I'm just nervous about the Expo," Ivy admitted.

"Well, I had an idea for another product," Amber said. "I want to make a windmill."

"A windmill?" Ivy asked, confused.

Amber dumped a handful of items onto the counter. Straws, skewers, craft sticks, rubber bands. It was the same bunch of stuff she'd been bringing to the library. Ivy hadn't realized she'd been working on an actual thing.

"But," Ivy pointed out. "REBELs Incorporated is supposed to be a toy company."

"Then it can be a toy windmill." Amber stuck parts together randomly. "Wind power for a greener future, Ivy. Wren's been really supportive of me doing it, but hadn't had a chance to help me figure it out. Now I'm not sure I'll get it done in time."

Kammie grabbed a straw and inspected it. "What does a windmill need?"

"It depends on what the windmill does." Amber pointed a skewer at her. "Some windmills used to pump water from the ground, and some would grind wheat into flour. Now-a-days windmills are used to make electricity."

Ivy perked up. "Hey, that's a great idea. Why don't we make it a model of a wind generator?"

"That's what Wren had suggested too," Amber said off-handedly. "I mean, we can make a pretend one, but we can't actually generate real electricity or anything, right?"

"Wren suggested it?" Ivy asked. "When was that? I don't remember that."

"Oh, yeah," Kammie nodded. "I think you were at basketball practice when we talked about it. You really should give her more credit, Ivy. She's a great boss. She makes me feel motivated and proud, and she comes up with the best ideas. She just gets a little lost when it comes to organizing and getting stuff done."

Ivy's mind spun. She replayed a lot of their meetings. It was true that everyone had a good time when Wren was around. She was so creative and funny. Maybe some of their problems weren't really Wren's fault at all. Was it the CEO's job to do all the little things or to see the big picture? Ivy pushed the thought aside. Wren wasn't here, and they had to get something done.

"I love the idea. Let's research," Ivy suggested.

Amber brought out the iPad, and they looked up *wind generator*. Apparently, industrial wind generators were super complicated. Who knew? But like most technology, they were built from many smaller, easier to understand parts. Almost every big, complicated problem or invention could be figured out if you just broke it down into smaller pieces, even electricity generators.

Electricity wasn't made by mixing ingredients together, like making a batch of cookies, or built by fastening pieces together like building a house. Electricity, a primal force, had to be collected, or "generated."

"Wren would probably say generating electricity was like summoning magic," Ivy thought, *"But instead of a wand and spells, you use technology."* Which actually made some sense. You use technology to collect, focus, and guide electricity the way a wizard might collect, focus, and guide magical energy with a magic wand. One was real and the other just a story, but the idea was the same.

According to the websites, most electricity generators worked by making something spin. Solar seemed to work differently, but most generators used wind, water, or burning coal to spin something around really fast. So that was the idea behind a windmill. Or a turbine, as they called it. The wind blew on the blades of the turbine, spinning it around like a pinwheel and turning a cylinder inside.

And that's where the magic happened. Interestingly, they seemed to use a lot of—

"Copper." Amber looked up at Ivy. "Most of these

homemade thingies use copper wire. Why copper? I mean, copper tape can be a great natural way to keep slugs and snails from eating my garden, but why use copper, specifically, in this case?"

Ivy skimmed the information on one of the webpages. "Copper is one of the best conductors, which means it's really good at holding and channeling electricity. But what I really want to know is why you need to spin something to make it."

"You don't already know?" Amber raised her eyebrows. "Don't you know everything about electricity?"

"No way," Ivy laughed. "I know some stuff about how to USE electricity, and how it behaves, but I've never studied how you generate it. Electricity and electronics are really complicated. There's always more to learn."

Kammie pointing to a diagram. "Says here it also involves magnets. That's weird. What do magnets have to do with electricity?"

Ivy typed *electricity, magnets,* and *copper wire* into the search bar. Meanwhile, Amber grabbed a paper straw and a skewer. She inserted the thin bamboo skewer into the straw. The skewer rattled around inside the significantly larger straw.

"Too loose," Amber mumbled. "I either need a thicker skewer or a thinner straw."

"What are you trying to do?" Asked Kammie.

"Put a shaft in a holder, so it can spin around like an axle. We'll stick the blades of the wind turbine on the shaft, and let it spin around inside the straw." Amber shook the straw and skewer. "I thought a skinny stick like a skewer would be perfect to attach the blades too, but this isn't working."

Kammie dug through the stuff on the counter and offered her a skinny coffee stirrer straw. Amber shoved the skewer in, but now it was too tight and wouldn't turn.

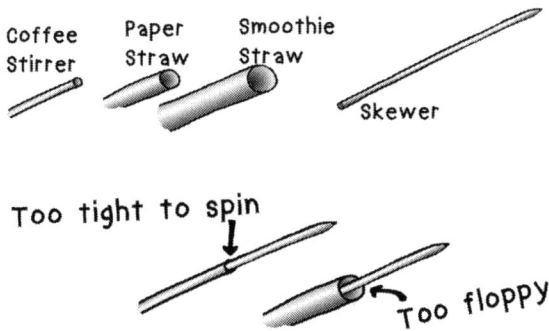

"What about an extra wide smoothie straw around the paper straw? Don't use the skewer at all." Kammie handed a fat straw to Amber, who slipped the smaller straw inside the larger one.

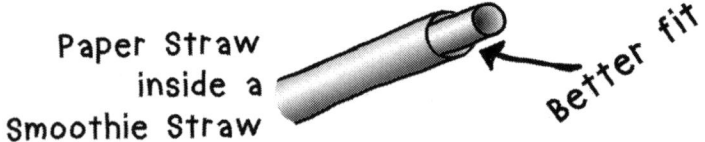

The paper straw didn't wobble as much, but could still spin around. It wasn't perfect, but it worked.

"Good enough. Now we just need fan blades and some kind of building to attach it to," Amber said.

Kammie held up a playing card. "How about this for the blades? It's stiff and strong and light. Oh! We could cut slots into the smaller straw and just slide it in the slots!"

Amber beamed. "You're brilliant!"

"Wren would have thought of it sooner," Kammie blushed. "I wonder where she is."

Amber tried to smile. "I'm sure she's fine. Trixie too. You know, I asked Trixie why she hasn't been coming to the Greenhouse lately. She just said her mom was still trying to teach her to read. She's really frustrated."

They shared another helpless look before Amber turned back to her invention. She cut the card in half, then folded each half in half and snipped part of the way across at the fold line.

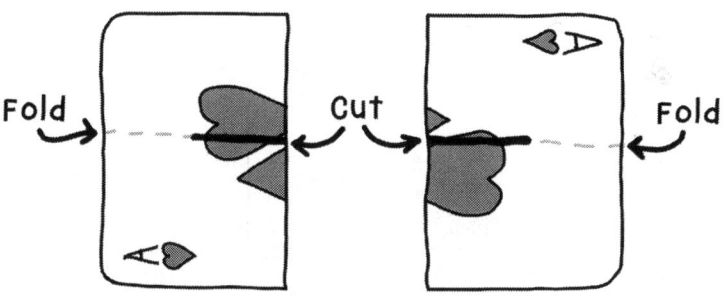

She slid them together at the cuts, inserting one cut into the other to make an X. Next, she took the paper straw and snipped four cuts into one end, lengthwise. Finally, she slipped the card X into the end of the straw.

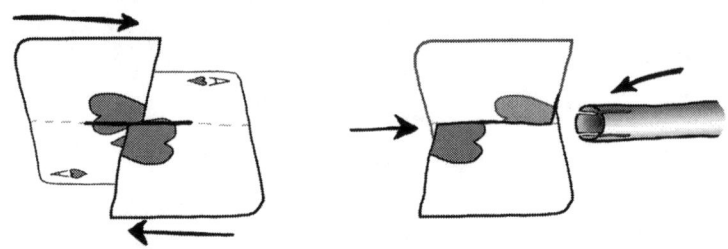

Amber twirled the X and straw between her palms. Kammie held up the smoothie straw and Amber dropped the whole paper straw apparatus into it.

She blew on the strips of card from the side. They rotated inside the smoothie straw like a pinwheel.

"Now we just need somewhere to put it. We can make a building out of cardboard that will hold the straws horizontal and high enough that the blades can spin." Amber grabbed some scrap cardboard and popped a hole wide enough for the smoothie straw in one of them. Then she just taped them together in a rectangle and slid the smoothie straw into the hole.

"It looks just like a windmill!" Kammie smiled. "Ivy, have you figured out how to make it generate electricity?"

Ivy scratched the back of her neck.

"This is really complicated," she said. "I mean, the theory isn't that hard to understand. You spin magnets around a lot of coiled copper wire, and it generates electricity. But in industrial generators, they have tons of other parts and all different kinds of metal. I guess that's to make it more efficient."

"Efficient?" asked Kammie. "I don't understand."

"It means you want to capture as much electricity as you can without wasting it," Ivy explained. "Like if you're making cookies, you want to use every part of the dough."

"Or eat it," Amber pointed out. "You scrape the bowl to get every last bit."

"Yeah, it's the same idea," Ivy nodded. "You want to use the right stuff to make sure none of your electricity disappears in the air. And none of the cookie dough disappears down the sink. And now I'm hungry."

Kammie looked confused. "That still doesn't explain how spinning magnets make electricity."

"Apparently, when the magnets spin, they pass under the copper wire one at a time, really fast."

"Okay," Kammie squinted. "And that makes electricity?"

"From what I can tell," Ivy explained. "The magnets sort of squeeze the electricity out of the copper. Or something like that, honestly I'm not really sure. The bottom line is that if you spin a bunch of magnets near copper wire, it generates electricity."

"So dirty stuff, like burning coal," Amber asked, "Uses the heat from the coal to turn the magnets, right?"

"And could you spin the wire instead of the magnets?" Kammie asked. "What about solar, does that use magnets and copper wire too?"

Ivy shrugged. "If we really want to know all the details, we should do more research, but these are great questions."

"Wait, renewable energy is starting to make more sense," Amber continued. "Wind and water turn the magnets by just their natural movement, so they aren't making a lot of smoke and waste and stuff."

"Yeah," Ivy nodded. "That makes sense. So at least in theory, if we hook your windmill blades there up to a disk with a bunch of magnets, and put a giant copper wire spool near it, we should be able to generate our own electricity!"

That, Ivy thought, would certainly be like magic.

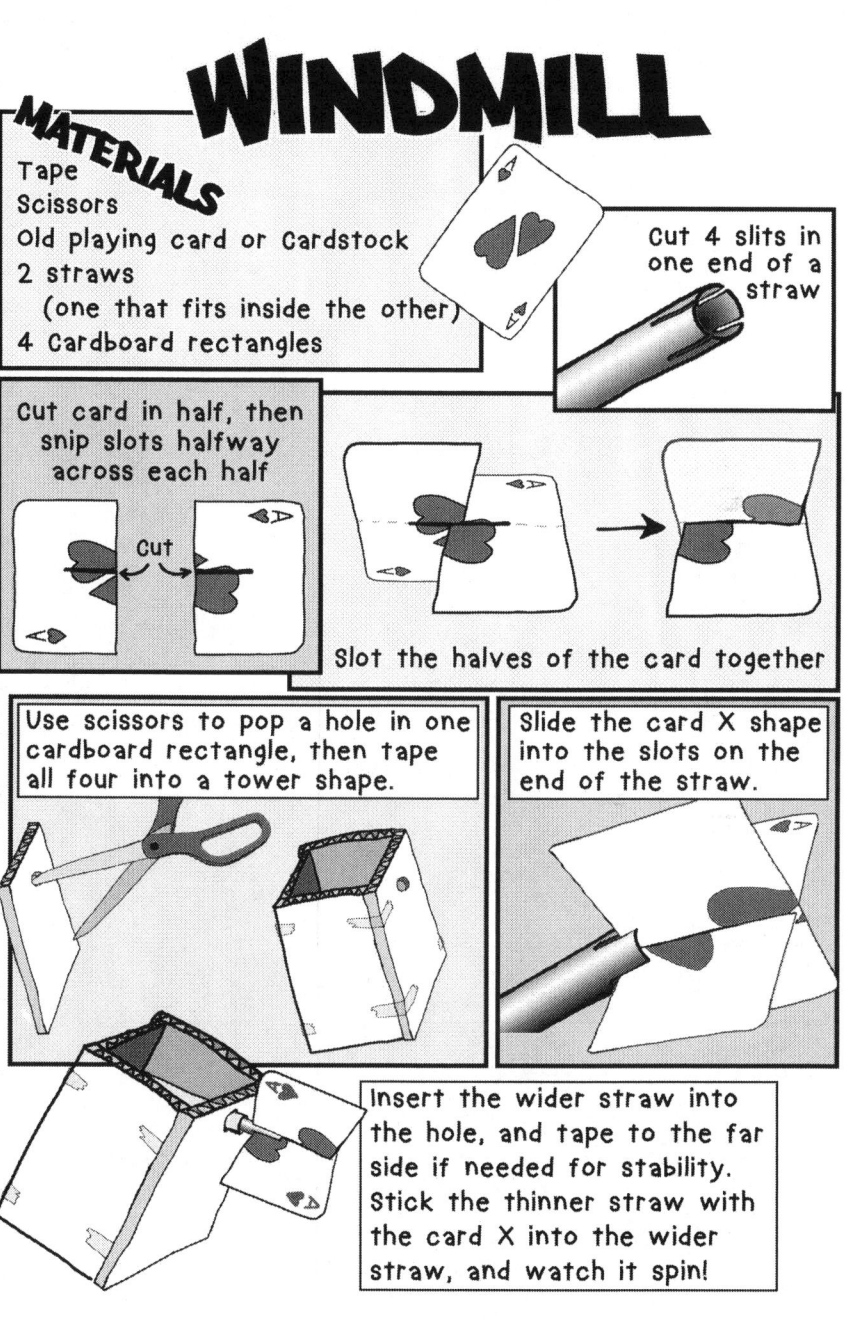

22
WREN

Ivy rushed off to her basketball game directly from Amber's, so she hadn't expected to hear from Wren at all on Saturday. But no one could reach Wren or her family all weekend. When she didn't show up for lunch on Monday, everyone was officially concerned.

Wren never missed lunch.

"She was in science class this morning," Amber speared a tomato with her fork, but didn't eat it. "We even did a hands-on experiment. But she hardly spoke to me at all. Then she rushed out of class before I could talk to her."

"What's going on with her?" Kammie played with her chips.

Ivy felt guilty. She didn't want Wren running their company anymore, but she didn't want her to disappear. And honestly she wasn't even sure about not running the company the more she learned about what Wren was actually doing for REBELs. All those little things Ivy hadn't noticed, like having a vision and inspiring the others.

Wren was her friend. She made them laugh, she always had their backs. Wren might be static electricity, but she was THEIR static electricity. No, not static. She was their lightning. And she was a pretty good leader, after all.

Ivy had always thought the most important goal of a company was to be successful, but Wren seemed to value the company's people and ideas over its success. And maybe, Ivy thought, maybe that wasn't such a bad way to run a company. Even if it might not get the attention of people like Dr. Caroline Kim.

"There she is!" Kammie yelled, surprising Ivy. Kammie never yelled.

A head of unruly mousey-brown hair trudged towards them through the boiling sea of kids on the playground. Wren flopped her lunch bag on the picnic table and sat on the bench instead of perching on the tabletop. Quietly, she pulled out a bagel, but didn't look at any of them.

"Hey Wren." Amber placed a gentle hand on her shoulder. "Where have you been?"

Wren cringed at the touch and didn't say anything.

Ivy tried to think of something supportive to say, blurting out the first thing that came to her mind. "Um, hey, did you read that book I gave you?"

Ivy cringed as Kammie and Amber stared at her. What a dumb thing to say. But Wren didn't even blink.

"I don't know," she said mechanically.

"I mean," Ivy thought fast. "You've been doing a really good job leading the company. I just thought you might have read it and it might have been helpful."

Amber narrowed her eyes at Ivy. Ivy shrugged helplessly and Amber rolled her eyes.

"I don't really care," Wren replied to her bagel. "Why don't you be CEO? I know you want to. It's better for everyone."

Ivy blinked.

"But... you're doing a great job," Ivy reassured her. And to her surprise, she actually meant it. "You were right, Wren. You are a good leader."

Wren shrugged. Kammie placed a gentle hand on her shoulder but Wren shook it off.

"Seriously," Ivy persisted. "You're doing a much better job than a lot of other companies' CEOs!"

Amber looked at Ivy from the corner of her eyes. "How do you know what the other companies are doing?" She asked.

Wren just shrugged. "It doesn't matter. Nothing matters."

"What happened, Wren?" Kammie asked quietly.

"I just don't care, okay?" Her eyes blazed behind a curtain of tears. "Everything you ever said about me is true, Ivy. I know what you've been thinking. I'm no good and none of it matters."

"Hey." A deep pit opened in Ivy's stomach. She'd been unfair. She needed to fix it. "That's no way for a CEO to think! Where's that Wren confidence! Come on, you can do it! We're all here to help you. Let's get organized, and we'll be the best company in the whole darn Expo!"

Ivy had meant to light the fire in her belly. Boost Wren's fighting spirit like a pump-up before a game. But instead, Wren folded onto herself like a flower in the frost. Then, she started crying. Her face scrunched up and turned red. Big, wet tears started to stream from her eyes as Wren's mouth twisted around the words she tried to get out. In all the years she'd known her, Ivy couldn't remember ever seeing Wren cry.

"You have no idea how hard I'm already trying," Wren sobbed, shoving her uneaten lunch back into her bag. "Just shut up. It doesn't matter. No matter how hard I try, nothing changes. I'm tired of trying. Everybody hates me no matter what I do. I give up. YOU be CEO Ivy. I'm serious. It's what you want and you think you can do a better job. You probably can. I'm tired of fighting."

She stood and grabbed her bag, yanking it off the table. She'd forgotten to zip it up. Bits of lunch spilled out. Her bagel landed open under the picnic table, cream cheese against the dirty ground. Wren stared at it, then squeezed her eyes shut, zipped up the remaining contents of her bag, and ran for the doors of the school, bumping blindly into a few of the older boys from Bobby and Milo's group who were shooting hoops.

The boys laughed at her as she ran.

"I'm sorry!" Ivy yelled after her. "What did I do?"

She turned to Amber and Kammie beseechingly. They

just shook their heads. Kammie picked up the bagel and threw it into the garbage.

"I was just trying to help," Ivy told them.

Amber glared at Ivy as she shoved her own lunch back into its bag. "I'm going to try and find her."

Ivy, frozen, just watched her go.

"Good luck!" She called. It was all she could think to do.

23

GIVING UP

"I was just trying to help," repeated Ivy.

Mr. Vincent droned on about the genius of Shakespeare. From the back of the class, Ivy kept an eye on the English teacher while trying to talk to Wren.

"I'm sorry if I said something wrong," Ivy tried again. "I really do think you're a good leader."

Mr. Vincent glanced their way. Ivy turned back to her book.

"Are you okay?" She whispered again.

Wren had washed her face, but it was still a little blotchy and the whites of her eyes were pink. But she stared straight ahead, as if she couldn't hear Ivy.

"I'm not mad at you," Wren finally whispered. "I'm just. I don't know. I'm just confused."

"About what?" Ivy asked.

"Shhhhhh," cautioned Milo, sitting behind them. Mr. Vincent glanced over again.

They were quiet for a few minutes as they learned about rhyming couplets.

"*So, till the judgement that yourself arise. You live in this, and dwell in lovers' eyes,*" Mr. Vincent recited importantly. "Sonnet fifty-five. Now if you look at page eighty-three…"

Ivy leaned over again as the teacher turned to write something on the whiteboard. "What do you mean? What are you confused about?"

Wren didn't say anything. She was copying down notes from the whiteboard. But Ivy continued to lean near her. Wren sighed.

"I'm just not a good person, okay?" She whispered even more quietly than usual. "I'm broken and that's all there is to it. You be CEO. I'm serious. There's no reason I should drag everyone else down."

Wren turned the page in her Shakespeare book and ran her finger down the lines. Then she looked back up attentively at Mr. Vincent. Ivy could hear pens and pencils skritching over notebooks around them as Mr. Vincent's monotonous voice droned on.

Ivy didn't know what to think. Was this change in Wren her fault? She'd tried to be a team player, but maybe hadn't insulated her disappointment very well. Maybe her feelings had zapped Wren's confidence.

But that didn't make sense. Whatever was going on with Wren was new. It had to be something about that second test. If Wren would just talk to them, the Renegades could help. That's what teams were for. Ivy had to find out.

"What happened over the weekend?"

Wren waved her away.

Behind them, Milo shushed again.

Mr. Vincent turned to the class with narrowed eyes, scanning the students. Ivy sat up straighter until he looked down at his book and started reading another Shakespearean sonnet.

She leaned over to Wren again. "You have to tell me. I can help. Look, we can work together on the business, there's no reason you have to step down as CEO. You're doing a good job. Sure, you stumbled around a bit at first, but that's just learning. You inspire people. You make stuff fun. You're a natural, just like you always said. Please talk to me."

A smile broke through Wren's gloomy face. Her eyes glistened with emotion.

"Thanks," Wren whispered. "But I might not be able to do REBELs at all anymore. It's for the best. I'm destined to mess things up. Thanks, really, but there's no hope for me."

"What?" Ivy spoke a little louder than she'd planned. "You can't quit. You're not a quitter."

Wren shrugged with a sad smile still on her face, and kept her eyes on her notes.

Mr. Vincent's head shot up. He looked directly at the girls.

"Wren!" he called. "Would you like to teach this class, young lady?"

She looked at him. "Huh? Um. No?"

"You seem to have a lot to say," Mr. Vincent snarled.

"No," Wren whimpered. "I didn't. I wasn't. It wasn't me! Please go on, I'm paying attention."

Several kids in the class groaned, and a few chuckled. Wren's face went red and she sunk down into her chair.

"Don't argue with me," Mr. Vincent said. "You were clearly talking. If you can't focus on class I'm going to have to send you to see Principal Sophie again."

"I was paying attention this time!" Wren wailed.

"Overreacting much?" Lily cough-talked. Emma stifled a laugh.

"No," Wren looked around frantically. "I was paying attention! It's not my fault."

"Calm down," Mr. Vincent directed. "Don't argue with me."

"See?" Wren cried. "I'm not even doing anything and I can't stay out of trouble."

Ivy thought about how upset Wren had been going into class in the first place, watching helplessly as she started breathing heavily. Some of the kids in class rolled their eyes, others sighed, and others whispered to each other. Milo, behind them, looked concerned. He reached out to Wren but was too far back. Wren's voice continued to escalate, spiraling into panic.

"Mr. Vincent," Ivy called. "It was my fault. I was the one talking. Wren was paying attention."

The Renegade Success Plan

The teacher looked doubtful. The other kids seemed to not even hear her.

"Really," Ivy insisted "She wasn't doing anything but telling me to be quiet."

"Well then if that's true, Ms. Park, please stop talking. You're disturbing the class," He still didn't look like he believed her.

"That's not fair," wailed Wren. "When you thought it was me, you got angry and screamed at me. With her you're all, 'please be quiet.' *WHY?*"

The class erupted in more giggles and eye rolls. Wren looked around desperately, breathing heavier, her eyes glazing over with terror. Milo began to stand up, but Wren was already on her feet.

"You all hate me! Stop it!"

She turned and ran from the room.

"You'd better be heading to Ms. Sophie's office, young lady," Mr. Vincent called after her, shaking his head. Then he mumbled under his breath. "She asks why she gets in trouble, then she pulls this kind of attitude again."

Ivy's stomach sank. She felt like she might throw up. Taking a deep breath, Ivy stood up as Mr. Vincent turned the page in his book. Before he could start class again, Ivy spoke up.

"Mr. Vincent. I really was the one who was talking—"

"She was!" Milo chimed in. He craned his neck towards the door, trying to see where Wren had gone.

"—If anyone should be sent to the principal's office, it's

me. Wren wasn't doing anything," Ivy insisted. "Can I please go find her?"

Mr. Vincent took a deep breath and let it out slowly.

"Please sit down, Ivy," he said calmly. "You will not leave this classroom until class is over. We are all familiar with your friend's hysterics. And while it's admirable you're trying to protect her, I will not have this class disrupted any longer. We have another sonnet to cover and the other kids in this classroom matter too. Now please turn to page eighty-six."

Ivy trembled slightly as she lowered herself into her seat. She'd seen Wren melt down before, and had always thought she was overreacting too. But seeing it from Wren's side, and knowing for a fact that she was the one responsible, gave her new insight. She suddenly saw the path that led to Wren's overloaded explosion. A path no one else had seen, that IVY had never seen before.

Now she saw it as clearly as a lightbulb on a dark night. Like a switch being flipped. All those times Wren had blown up, gotten in trouble, overreacted... She wasn't trying to be difficult. She wasn't choosing to be oppositional. Wren wasn't trying to give anyone a hard time. She was HAVING a hard time. Wren was struggling and no one was listening to her.

It was like Wren suddenly switched to a different language, like she didn't have the words to explain what was inside her head. It looked like she was a jerk. But she wasn't. She was trying so hard, Ivy could see that now.

But it was too late.

24

APTITUDE

"This isn't what I expected," Amber squinted at the results from her aptitude test. "What does ESFP mean?"

Ivy looked down at her own aptitude test results. The students had finally gotten them that morning, and now they clustered around the library tables discussing them with each other.

They were confusing.

Instead of a profession, the printouts listed numbers and letters. Hers talked about whether she was an extrovert or an introvert, thinking or feeling, and a bunch of other ideas that didn't seem to have much to do with a career. The summary section didn't just say "you should be an electrical engineer." Instead, there were thick paragraphs of strengths and weaknesses, personality types, and types of jobs you might be interested in. Nothing concrete.

Interpreting and reading the results took valuable time. And time was in short supply.

They only had a few days left before the Expo. Businesses all over the school were falling apart under the stress of the upcoming deadline. It was easy to think up a business idea, but much more complicated to flesh it out with other people. To make it actually happen. At the next table over, Bobby slammed a book down in front of one of the other boys and yelled at him.

Kammie jumped.

Over at Axel's table, on the other hand, the robot danced around while her team literally patted each other on the back. Coderville ran like a well-oiled machine.

Much better than REBELs Incorporated. Wren wasn't there and it didn't look like she was coming. Amber gave up on trying to decode her aptitude test and tossed it on the table.

"I'm going to go find Wren," Amber stood up. "She owes us some answers."

Kammie poured over her own test results. "What does this even mean? I'd do well with a project based, self-motivated career involving logical thinking?"

"I have no idea," Ivy folded a tall tower out of some teal cardstock, the same color as their favorite infinity block. She wanted to make the body of their wind generator more attractive, like it was part of their line of toys.

Amber had brought in the whole windmill. It sat on the table as Ivy sized up where to put the folds. Since the cardstock wasn't very strong, she planned on just covering their existing tower with the attractive paper. Ivy taped the cardstock into place as the library door creaked open.

Amber reappeared, dragging a frowning Wren over to their table.

"Sit." Amber pointed to a chair.

Wren sat.

"How are you?" Kammie asked.

Wren didn't answer.

"Okay look," Ivy crossed her arms. "The Expo is on Friday. If you don't want to tell us what's going on, that's okay, but we only have a few days left. Let's get through it together. No quitting this close to the finish line."

"Oh FINE," Wren huffed. "But I'm not agreeing to any sort of leadership."

"Why's that?" Coach Bakes appeared over Amber's shoulder. "You guys are doing a great job."

"I just want Ivy to take over," Wren grumped. "Is that okay? Can we do that?"

The coach tapped her lips thoughtfully. "I don't see why not. But why don't you want to take your team over the finish line?"

Wren looked down. "My sister and I got called back for more testing."

"Ah," the coach sat in an empty seat next to her. "I see."

Ivy, Kammie, and Amber shared a look. What did the coach know that they didn't?

"I don't understand," Ivy said. "Why would they need to test aptitude more than once in a row? At first, I thought maybe they couldn't figure out what career to pigeonhole Wren into and needed some more information. But these results don't list a career recommendation. Just a bunch of stuff about personality."

The coach nodded but didn't take her eyes off Wren. "Aptitude tests are tests to see if you're suited for a particular job. They aren't crystal balls that tell your future. These were more like assessment tests. They include a lot of different ways to get insight into a person. They aren't clinical or anything, but were supposed to help you all understand your personality types, your temperament, your strengths and weaknesses and interests, all the things you want to consider when you're choosing a career. The idea was for you to talk to your parents about the results. Open a conversation."

Ivy looked at her results page again. "Oh, that makes more sense."

"The test also screened for a number of things," Coach Bakes continued. "A screening identifies red flags. People who are at high risk for whatever they're looking for."

The table got quiet.

"And what were they looking for?" Kammie asked.

"Several things," the coach looked at Wren again. "Including learning and behavioral differences. That's it, isn't it, Sterling?"

Wren cringed, then nodded. "They say my sister has dyslexia."

"Trixie?" Amber gasped. "Is that why she's having so much trouble learning to read?"

Wren nodded. "I guess it's pretty bad. They say a lot of kids don't get diagnosed until they're older. So Mom says we were lucky to find out now."

"Wait. That doesn't make sense," Ivy said. "There's nothing wrong with Trixie. She's a smart kid."

Coach Bakes ran a hand through her hair. She chose her words with precision. "Dyslexia doesn't have anything to do with how smart you are. It's how your brain figures out language. Reading is really hard for a dyslexic person. Sometimes the letters seem to swim or flip around. Try reading a book when the letters won't sit still. Dyslexic people's brains just work a little differently. There are good things about a dyslexic brain, too."

"Yeah?" Wren looked up at her. "Like what?"

"Dyslexic people can excel at creative stuff. They're really good at seeing the big picture, and better at recognizing patterns and solving problems than people with typical brains. A lot of things. And speaking of businesses, did you know something like one out of every three entrepreneurs is dyslexic?"

"Really?" Ivy gaped. "That's a lot!"

"How do you know so much?" asked Wren.

The coach lifted her head proudly. "Because I'm dyslexic."

No one knew what to say, but Wren smiled for the first time all day.

"I'm gonna tell Trixie," she said. "It might cheer her up. She's been kind of angry, or sad, or something. I don't think she knows how she feels."

"That makes sense." The coach nodded. "It's tough to figure out how to feel when you find out you're different. On one hand, you finally have some answers, and on the other hand, you have a whole slew of new questions. And you have to figure out who you are all over again."

"Trixie must be really confused," Amber said quietly. "How did she get dyslexia?"

"That comes from your family. Genetics. Have you guys studied genetics yet?"

"So Trixie got her dyslexia from my parents? But they aren't dyslexic," Wren pointed out.

"And why did they test you?" Ivy asked Wren. "You're obviously not dyslexic. You read like seven hundred books a day. So what were they testing you for?"

Wren squirmed and looked away.

"The tests weren't just screening for dyslexia," the coach answered, still watching Wren. "There's all sorts of ways brains can be different. It's like with hair. Most people in the world are born with brown or black hair. But some people have hair that's definitely blonde, or like Rosenberg over here, red. And some people have hair in between. It's hard to tell if it's light brown or dark blonde, but what you call it doesn't change the color of the hair. You can have straight hair or curly hair or wavy hair. You take care of curly hair differently than straight hair, and thick hair differently than fine hair. There's nothing wrong with any hair, right? It's just hair. It just depends on what you're born with."

Coach Bakes ruffled her own short light brown hair

with a smile. She paused to let the girls think about what she was saying. Wren listened, her eyes wide and eager.

"And just like with hair, different brains run in families. It's not always the same kind of difference, but it's all related," the coach leaned forward, talking faster. She'd obviously done a lot of research on the topic. "They call it *neurodivergent*. *Neuro* means nerves or brain, and *divergent* means different. So *neurodivergent* is just a big, fancy, long word to mean people with different brains."

"What kinds of people?" Wren drank in every word.

"All kinds. You can have more than one difference in a brain, like your hair can be red AND curly AND thick. Autism, ADHD, dyslexia, OCD, dysgraphia..."

"I don't even know what some of those are," Wren interrupted. She looked at Amber and they both shrugged.

"Well, the links between dyslexia and ADHD, and ADHD and autism, are pretty high, but it's all hereditary. Genes. It all runs in families."

A loud noise came from the table next to them.

"We're not doing it that way and that's final!" Bobby shouted at one of the other boys.

"Excuse me, I have to go handle this," The coach stood up, scowling. "Some things aren't neurological differences at all, some things are just bad behavior. And hormones. Never underestimate the power of hormones. Why I decided to teach middle school kids, I'll never understand."

As Coach Bakes approached the next table, the boys immediately quieted down. She stood over Bobby and glared at them all. "It's time to get to business, boys."

Ivy had to agree, they had a business to run.

Wren didn't seem like she wanted to talk about her own tests. It sounded like Wren had a lot to process, and Ivy didn't want to push, despite her curiosity. Hopefully, she'd tell them about it when she was ready and, if not, they could encourage her after the Expo. The best thing to do now was get back to business. Wren wanted Ivy to be the CEO now, and she was up to the challenge, but she'd have to hustle.

"Let's figure out where we are," Ivy tried to sound like an authority. "Wren, why don't you go get our paperwork, and we'll get everything sorted."

Wren ran to their cubby and brought back a messy stack of paper. She set the pile in the middle of the table. Pages slid off in all directions. Ivy lifted one and another piece of paper, paperclipped to the edge, came with it. The second paper was paperclipped to another, which was paperclipped at a different place to a third, creating a chain of paper from Ivy's hand to the tabletop.

Ivy sighed, pulling the whole disorganized mess in front of her. She'd have to stay late tonight to get this all sorted out. But everything was within her control now. If she worked hard enough, did well enough, she might be able to impress Caroline after all. The ball was in her court.

Time to run with it.

25

PERMITS

The last kids left, squabbling about their marketing plan. Ivy sat alone in the library, still sifting through papers. The final bell rang and through the heavy library door, Ivy heard the muted sounds of kids calling to each other as they headed home for the evening.

Basketball practice would start in thirty minutes, but Ivy still shuffled through the messy stack of papers, trying to make sense of them. They didn't seem to be organized at all, and no one was around for her to ask if she had any questions.

Amber had Hebrew or her internship or something, Kammie had another zoom with her mom, and who knows what Wren was doing but she couldn't stay.

It was up to Ivy.

The librarian, the only other person in the whole library, looked at her watch. Apparently all the other companies were done, whatever "done" even meant. And honestly, REBELs could probably open on Friday without any more work.

But it wasn't enough.

Ivy still hoped, deep inside, that she might shake hands with Caroline Kim. That it would be her, not Axel, that earned her praise. It had seemed like such a sure thing not long ago, then it seemed impossible, and now, the shimmering, tempting tendrils of possibility taunted her. It could still happen.

She kept sorting through the business papers; their business plan, filled out with Kammie's neat handwriting, a revenue forecast, receipt copy of their business license application, the request for a permit for space at the Expo—

Wait.

The form requesting their table space for the Expo. Here in her hands. Not a signed receipt, but the original.

Wren never turned it in.

Without this form, they couldn't get a table at the Expo. Their entire business wouldn't happen. They wouldn't get any credit for it. They might even get in serious trouble with their teachers. An icy chill washed over Ivy.

She stared at the paper as realization dawned, breathing heavily. The form was all filled in properly. It was ready to go, there at the bottom of the stack of already completed papers. It must have gotten lost, Wren must have forgotten about it. How do you forget about something so important?

Ivy scanned the instructions. "Due no later than Thursday morning before the Entrepreneurial Expo," it said. "Table location is first come, first served." Today was Tuesday and every minute wasted meant a table further in the back, where no one could find them.

"Excuse me?" She called to the librarian, waving the paper. "Who do I turn this in to?"

The librarian was packing her purse impatiently. "Is that for a table? You can turn it in at the office. Look, I have to head out. Are you almost done here? I'm not supposed to leave you unsupervised, but I have an appointment to get to."

The office was just around the corner.

"Sure," Ivy nodded. "I'm just waiting for basketball practice to start. I'll just be another few minutes and can turn this in on my way out."

"The office is closing in, like, 2 minutes." The librarian looked at her watch again. "Tell you what. Why don't you go drop that off now before they leave, and then come get your stuff. You'll be fine, right? You don't need anything from me?"

Ivy was already heading for the door, walking as fast as she could.

"Sure, thanks, no problem." She yanked the door open. "Thanks!"

Principal Sophie was just turning the key in the office door as Ivy rushed up.

"Wait!" she called. "Can I turn this in? Please? Sorry it's late!"

The principal, a small, well dressed woman about the same age as Ivy's mom, looked at the clock on the wall.

"Just in time, Ms. Park. In another minute it would have been too late for this evening, and you would have had to try and catch me tomorrow. Rules are rules." She accepted the paper and slipped it into an envelope on her secretary's desk. "You're turning it in awfully late. I'm afraid your table will be near the back."

Ivy sighed. Yet another setback. "Yeah, sorry. Wren kept saying she was going to turn it in. I guess she just forgot."

Ms. Sophie paused with her key in the office door again. "Wren? Sterling?"

Ivy nodded.

"I see," she finished locking the door and withdrew the key. "That's understandable then. I'm glad we found out now so we can help her. She's got a good heart, that one. It all makes so much sense now."

"What makes sense?" Ivy perked up. "Is it the second testing? She won't tell us anything."

Principal Sophie blinked. "Oh dear, I'm so sorry. I spoke out of turn. I assumed she'd tell you since you're one of her closest friends. But it's her choice, of course."

"Tell me what?" Ivy had to get back to the library or she'd be late for practice, but this might be her chance to help Wren. "Please, Ms. Sophie. Please tell me what happened."

But the principal just shook her head. "I'm sorry, I can't disclose personal information. Rules are rules even for best friends. Please talk to her if you want to know more. Now, run along. I'm closing up here and you shouldn't be in the building alone. What are you doing here so late?"

Ivy's shoulders drooped. The stern and unyielding principal would never budge. She had a reputation as a stickler for the rules.

"I just have to grab my stuff from the library and head to basketball practice. I guess I'll sort out the rest of the paperwork at home after dinner. Thank you for taking the application."

The hallway back to the library was quiet and dark. Ivy plodded back to the library, everything she had to do spinning through her head. She pushed the door open like it weighed a thousand pounds. But she couldn't give up. She just couldn't. What would that make her? If she didn't give it her all, wouldn't that make her a quitter?

She'd been bringing everything she had to her basketball games and they were on the verge of becoming champions. A testimony to what happened when you applied the right effort. At least she could feel like a success at her basketball games.

Ivy gathered the stack of remaining papers together. She should bring them home and finish them after dinner, but she was so tired. Instead of sticking the paperwork in her backpack, she brought it to the dark alcove with the cubbies. With the lights out, it was even darker back there than usual. *And no one from any other business is here,* Ivy thought bitterly, *because they all got everything done on time. Darn it Wren, why couldn't you do a better job?*

She reached into the front pocket of her backpack and pulled out the code thrower. It might never be part of their toy product line, but at least it would give her some light right now.

The little contraption felt heavier than it should. As she pulled it out, Ivy saw the key to Axel and Emma's cubby, dangling from the light by a loose bit of electrical tape.

Ivy scowled at it. Axel's team was doing so well. She'd be the one shaking Caroline's hand for sure. They probably even got a prime location for their table.

Ivy slammed her own cubby door shut after stuffing in the papers. Then she paused, looking at the key.

That glorious, impressive robot. Did Coderville deserve it? They didn't even know how it worked, they just wrote code for it. They were going to win based on technology they didn't even understand.

Somewhere in the back of her mind, a small voice that sounded a lot like Kammie reminded Ivy that there were no winners in the Expo. But it lied. There were always winners. And there were always losers. And Ivy wasn't used to being a loser. She didn't like it.

Ivy looked around the dark library. Nobody was there.

Without even knowing what her body was doing, Ivy found her hand lifting the key to the lock on Axel's cubby door. She rested the weight of her hand on it for a moment. What was she doing? It wouldn't make any difference that this robot from Sapai Industries would steal the show. Axel deserved to win. She'd done a great job. They all had.

But did they? Did they deserve to win if they didn't even understand what they were doing? They weren't a robotics company, they were coding the robot. But Ivy UNDERSTOOD. And Coderville would beat her to a prize they didn't even care about anyway. They weren't hoping to impress the CEO of Sapai Industries. Axel probably didn't even know she was going to be at the Expo. Axel hadn't read *Success Plan*, Axel hadn't emailed Dr. Kim. Axel wasn't on a first name basis with Caroline.

And yet Axel would be the one shaking her hand. Ivy couldn't think of anything at this point that she could do to help REBELs win. Not really. She could give herself all the pep talks in the world. She'd do her best, but they were too far behind, and their table at the Expo was going to be way back in some dark corner. Even if she could somehow add another killer product to their line-up, no one would ever see them. Coderville was going to steal the show.

Ivy opened Axel's cubby. The robot's smooth white body sat still and quiet in the shadows. She turned it around to expose the circuitry in the back, the wires and jumpers that controlled its various body parts. Ivy understood how each connection would make the robot's arms and legs move, like reading a book. Her eyes traced how the energy would flow along each path. There wasn't a person on Axel's team who understood it like Ivy did.

She reached in and slid a jumper off its pins. The tiny piece of plastic and metal could be slipped over two itty bitty metal rods that were mounted on the motherboard, creating a connection, routing or rerouting the flow of electricity. If Ivy changed the jumper's position just a little, the connection would go somewhere else. Like a train track that had been switched to an adjoining track.

She put the jumper in a different position. Just like that. The robot wouldn't work anymore. Then what would they do? Then they'd have to learn about the technology. They'd have to earn their win.

Ivy puffed out a deep breath. She needed to calm down. In fact, she needed to get to practice. She'd really be in trouble if Coach Bakes came looking for her. It didn't even feel that wrong anymore. First just a little look in someone else's cubby to answer one question, then deeper looks, more cubbies. Now here she was, actually messing with someone else's product. Getting caught here, with her hand literally inside someone else's cubby, would be hard to explain. There'd be no talking her way out of trouble if—

"Park!" a familiar voice barked. It did not sound happy. "That doesn't look like your cubby."

Ivy slammed the door shut. The coach stared at her with electricity shooting out of her eyes. Her mouth was a small angry knot, and her cheeks flushed.

"You're late for practice."

26

BUSTED

"I— I—" Ivy stammered. She reached up and locked the cubby, then withdrew the key.

"How did you get that key?" growled the coach.

Ivy looked down at the key in her hand. Its outlines blurred. A rushing noise filled her head. She couldn't think of anything to say. Nothing at all. Not a single thought came into her head. She looked up with terrified eyes into the coach's rage.

"Spying again?" Coach Bakes stared at her. "And you were doing more than just spying this time, weren't you?"

Ivy's breath came faster. The room began to wobble under her feet. She should just tell the coach the truth. *Come clean, Ivy,* she urged her frozen mouth. *Just come clean and tell her you made a mistake.* It was the right thing to do.

But—

If she admitted to sabotage, Ivy would get thrown out

of the Expo. And everyone would know why. Everyone would know Ivy Rose Park was a cheater. Then what would happen to her success plan? What would Caroline think if she knew? No more first-name status. Never another email. Forget that handshake. The coach had no proof. No one else would ever see the tiny little change to a single little jumper.

Ivy swallowed, took a breath, and looked the coach in her eyes. "No ma'am. I was just checking to make sure the robot was okay."

"Now lying too?" After a moment, Coach Bakes sighed. "I expect better from my team. I expect better from you, Park. I'm disappointed in you. Very disappointed."

"I understand. I won't do it again," Ivy nodded. She wanted nothing more than to put this moment behind her and get on the basketball court. To run some drills with Emma and forget she'd ever opened this stupid cubby door. She pledged to herself to actually never do it again. Her corporate espionage days were over.

"Well, if you do do it again, it won't be my problem," Coach Bakes shook her head. "You're off the team, Park."

Ivy's head shot up. She stared at the coach in disbelief, speechless.

"Out of respect to your teammates in your Expo group, and because I have no hard evidence, I'm not going to report this to Ms. Sophie. We will say you quit the team because you have too much going on and your priorities are elsewhere. That's true enough," Coach Bakes continued.

"You've put me in a difficult situation, and now your fellow Machines will have to pick up your slack."

"But you CAN'T!" Ivy cried. "It's not fair!"

Coach Bakes leveled a look of deep disapproval on her, "Fair?"

"Yes!" The air in the library felt heavier. The walls closed in around Ivy. "It's not fair to them, it's not fair to me! I've worked so hard. I'm the best player on the team and you know it. I've put in so much work, sacrificed so much you don't even know. You can't kick me off now, not before the last few big games! What will the team think? That I can't cut it? That I'm weak?"

Coach Bakes crossed her arms over her chest, eyes hard, mouth set in a frown. "There's more than one way to be weak, Park. There's no shame in having limits. People aren't meant to be perfect. What you've shown tonight is far more concerning to me. You've shown a weakness of character. You've made bad decisions. You're not playing fair. There are repercussions for cheating—"

"WHAT?" Ivy sobbed. "I'm not—"

"Yes, cheating. I don't know what you'd call it in the corporate world, but in my world, stealing another team's plays is cheating. Not to mention whatever else you've done. The repercussions for cheating are serious, Park. I'm not opening MY team, my good team full of good athletes, I'm not opening them up to that kind of influence. On my team, Park, we play fair and we win fair." the coach shook her head. "You're off the team."

Coach Bakes turned and walked away. She didn't even look back.

Ivy collapsed against the wall of cubby doors. She slid down and plopped on the floor, tossing her stupid flashlight code thrower at a nearby trash can without even paying attention to its trajectory. It soared in a graceful arch and landed square inside. All net.

Ivy buried her head in her arm, and began to cry.

"I still don't understand why you needed to be picked up early," her mom said as Ivy threw herself into the passenger seat. "Practice usually runs much later. You've thrown off my schedule."

Ivy didn't answer. Her lips trembled as she stared straight ahead.

"Fine then, don't tell me." Her mom sighed.

They rode in silence for a few minutes. Finally, Ivy spoke in a soft voice.

"I'm not," she swallowed. "I'm not on the team anymore."

Her mom's eyes shot to her in surprise, then she turned them back to the road. "You quit the team? That's a surprise. You should have talked to me about it first."

Ivy didn't correct her.

Trudging up the stairs to their flat, Ivy realized she hadn't brought the paperwork home. And she'd finished all her homework at lunch because she thought she'd be at practice. It wasn't even her night to make dinner. Finally, some time with nothing to do, and she'd have to spend it figuring out what to tell the other Renegades. What to tell her mom.

Her mom headed to the kitchen to start cooking. Ivy threw herself onto her bed, with nothing to do for the rest of the evening but replay her choices over and over again in her head. If only she hadn't opened that cubby. If only she hadn't lingered. If only Wren had turned in the form.

If only she hadn't touched that robot.

No matter how hard she tried to think about something else, she just kept seeing all her mistakes. Over and over, all evening, during a sullen, silent dinner where her mom eventually stopped trying to engage her in conversation. After dinner doing nothing but staring at her ceiling. Spying, sabotage, cheating, lying, getting caught, getting kicked off the team. Her whole future, going down in flames a lot worse than not impressing Dr. Kim. And it was her own fault. Bad choices, bad luck, bad consequences looped over and over like a terrible show she couldn't turn off. Until finally, she fell asleep.

And dreamed about them.

27

CAROLINE

"Integrity," Dr. Caroline Kim stood in front of the entire school at Wednesday morning's assembly. Her clear, confident voice echoing through the gym. "It's never too late to do the right thing."

Ivy slumped down next to Wren, who sat up straight, drinking in every word. She nudged Ivy with her elbow.

"This is it, right?" Wren gushed. "This is what you've been waiting for! Sit up. Here, can you see okay?"

Ivy could see fine. Caroline stood tall and proud. Her energy would be visible even to people who didn't idolize her. As she spoke, Ivy couldn't help but visualize waves of power emanating from her. She was like some otherworldly force. Not a circuit, a power generator. Electricity danced around her, surrounding her as if she were a hero in a Marvel movie, but in a business suit instead of a funny costume.

"Success comes from being true to yourself. You are

successful when you let your inner fire burn and use it to fuel others. To be the best, you have to beat the best. No shortcuts. Otherwise, you can't call yourself the best. You can't call yourself successful."

Ivy had hoped that Caroline would say something meaningful to Ivy's life when she came to talk to the school. Now, she wished she wasn't hitting the target with so much accuracy. Ivy squirmed as Caroline kept going.

"Any successful business has all kinds of people in it. There are organizers and idea generators. There are people who can buckle down and make ideas happen. People who have had different struggles, lived all kinds of different lives, have complementary strengths and weaknesses. All of these kinds of people are like components," Caroline continued. "Each is important to the success of a device. And they need a motherboard, they need an operating system to help keep track of the big picture, to guide them and make the big picture decisions. Or to say it another way, the best lineman or running back isn't going to win without a good coach who can see their strengths and how that strength integrates into the whole team. They need a leader. They need a boss. They need someone to bring it all together. A boss isn't better than their team, a boss brings out the best in all of them."

She paused and looked over the crowd.

"If you want to be successful, learn about people. Your company is made of people. How they work, what motivates them, how people work best in groups. Learn how to talk to people who are different than yourself, and most importantly, learn how to disagree respectfully. See another's point of view and then share yours. Respectfully."

Ivy swallowed hard. She thought about the problems she'd been having with Wren. Had she been respectful? Had she truly listened?

"Just like electricity or magnets, people have a positive or negative charge. You have to figure out where you fit. What does success mean to you? And what will you do to be a positive charge in your business?"

The students gave Caroline a standing ovation. Even Wren clapped and whooped. Ivy hadn't seen her this lively since before she went in for that second test.

It brought a smile to Ivy's face.

The speech left her feeling inspired. She got to her feet with the rest of the kids, energized, ready to take on the world. This was why she loved Dr. Caroline Kim. She was inspirational.

Mr. Vincent tried to get everyone's attention above the fray, but everyone ignored him. Wren smiled a smile full of classic Wren mischief. She elbowed Ivy, bent her head towards the struggling Mr. Vincent, and raised a finger to her lips.

Then, with a wink, she disappeared into the crowd. Mr. Vincent rolled up a stack of papers like a bullhorn and yelled through it. Everyone still ignored him, shoving each other and calling to kids in other groups. He threw his arms up in frustration.

Where had Wren gone? Ivy, towering over the kids around her, scanned the heads in the crowd for a messy mop of light brown hair, but there were too many heads. Some teachers managed to gather their kids and march them back to class. Mr. Vincent wasn't one of them.

Wren had disappeared. Ivy thought she caught a glimpse of her over by the podium, but that was all the way on the other side of the room. Caroline leaned over to talk to someone, but Ivy couldn't see who it was. Just then, Mr. Vincent stood on top of the bleachers, cupped his hands around his mouth, and bellowed for his class to line up, counting students. Ivy was just lining up when Wren suddenly appeared again.

"Where did you go?" Ivy asked.

Wren just smiled at her. "You'll see."

Even later as they headed into the library at lunch to work more on their toys, Wren still wouldn't say anything.

As Ivy pulled out the paperwork, she heard voices getting louder from Axel's table.

"But WHY won't it work?" Emma yelled. "What did you do? It was working fine yesterday!"

Ivy cringed when she saw Axel's desperate expression. The blonde girl didn't answer. She just stabbed the enter key on her laptop over and over again.

"Who wrote the last piece of code?" Tyrone frantically scrolled through his own laptop. "Let's go through it line by line. Come on, this is somebody's fault."

Axel started hitting her return key again.

The other members of the team stared at the unmoving robot and bickered among themselves about how they might be able to get a replacement robot in time for Friday's Expo. One of them suggested a replacement CEO. Ivy turned away as Axel's face got red.

At another table, Milo leafed through his company's paperwork.

"This one didn't get filled out either! Did anybody do any work at all? Come on you guys, this affects our grades, stop messing around." He tossed the page on top of a growing pile in the middle of their table. Then, with a gasp, he waved another at his team. "Oh my gosh, this is the application for a table at the Expo! It's due Thursday morning!"

All over the library, teams yelled at each other, or frantically rustled through their paperwork, or rushed to finish merchandise. Ivy had to imagine there were also a lot of teams that had it together, that weren't falling apart under the stress of the deadline. But those kids weren't here at the last minute. Every company in the library seemed to be in trouble. And time was running out.

28

THE RIGHT THING

*I*vy closed her eyes.

It was time for action, the last chance, the final push. Otherwise known as Wednesday. The Wednesday before the Friday of the Expo. They still had time to pull out a miracle. Throw a Hail Mary pass. She just had to light that fire, get that electricity sparking again. Now that she'd heard Caroline speak, Ivy wanted to meet her more than ever. Wanted Caroline to be proud of her. It seemed silly to want a stranger to be proud of you, but there it was.

She'd made mistakes. She never should have spied on the other teams. It shouldn't have gone as far as it did. It wasn't harmless. But could she let a few mistakes define her future?

Sometimes a mistake was the best way to learn. You had to make the mistake to understand why it was a mistake. And some decisions that had bad consequences weren't mistakes at all, they just didn't work out the way you wanted them to. Sometimes it was hard to tell a good choice from a bad choice until you'd actually made it. And then it seemed like it was too late.

Axel had made a mistake at the beginning of the year, and Ivy had judged her for it. Now she understood it wasn't that simple. Ivy had made the same mistake, and paid the price of being thrown off her winning team, of being forced to abandon her teammates in shame and missing out on the successes she'd spent a lot of time and energy and hope helping create. But her price was at least a lot less public than what Axel had to pay.

All Ivy could do now was move forward. Learn the lesson. Make things right. The first step was to take the first step. REBELs had a lot of positives, Ivy wanted to concentrate on that. Take stock.

"What are our assets?" Ivy asked.

"We have these inventions," Wren pointed out.

The wind turbine model looked nice with its new cardstock cover. Amber, Wren, and Kammie played with the completed Infinity Blocks, sliding them across the table and trying to click the magnets together. Sometimes the blocks connected, and sometimes they would push away from each other instead. It looked fun.

"We have our paperwork all filled out, right?" Kammie suggested.

Kammie had gone through each form methodically,

making sure every question was answered, every paper completed.

"Oh wait," she said, leafing through the sheets, I filled this one out twice."

Kammie brought the extra sheet over to the trash can and suddenly gasped.

"How did this get in there?" Kammie pulled the code thrower out of the trash. She set the device on the table near the wind turbine. "So I guess we have this too."

Ivy looked away. She'd have to admit what she'd done at some point, but right now wasn't the time. Now was the time to put her mistakes aside and be the CEO for her company and her friends. For her only team left.

As if reading her mind Amber added, "and we have each other."

Before Caroline's speech, Ivy hadn't really thought about the team as assets, but they were. Wren had done a great job giving each of them something they enjoyed and were good at. She'd used everyone's skills and as a result, built a solid company. Everyone felt valued and invested. *Agency*, Caroline had called it. They felt *agency*. That meant they felt like they had meaningful control over what they were working on, that what they did MATTERED.

Ivy could learn that lesson in leadership from Wren. While she was at it, Amber could teach her a thing or two about loyalty and being honest, while Kammie had been totally right about following the rules.

Ivy glanced over at Coderville. Axel and Emma poured

over manuals. Tyrone typed furiously at his laptop. None of them smiled anymore. Things weren't going well for them. It wasn't their fault, of course, but instead of banding together, they were turning on each other. Any team could be a good team when they were. The true test of leadership and teamwork came from times when there were problems. And it didn't look like Axel's team was doing very well on that test.

Ivy stood up.

"Where are you going?" Amber asked.

Ivy pointed to the robot. "I need to go talk to them."

"That's really nice to help them out," Amber said over the blocks she was playing with.

Ivy took a deep breath as she approached the three kids and their silent, unmoving robot. Before she could say anything, Emma stood up. She blocked Ivy from the robot the way she might block a player from a shot.

"What are you doing here?" Emma sounded angry.

"I think I can help you guys," Ivy pointed to the robot.

Axel glanced up.

"You've done enough," Emma crossed her arms.

Did she know what Ivy had done to the robot? What else could she be talking about?

"Are you abandoning your own Expo team the way you abandoned the Lovelace Machines?" Emma raised her eyebrows. "You can't join Coderville. We don't allow traitors in this company."

Basketball. That's what Emma was mad about. With good reason, Ivy thought. The team had been doing so well, and now they'd lost their star player.

"I'm sorry, Emma," Ivy apologized. "I didn't want to quit the team."

"More important things to do, huh?" Emma sniffed. "Practice yesterday sucked. We're gonna get massacred this weekend. Coach is putting in Isabelle. ISABELLE, Ivy. And it's your fault."

Ivy sighed. She had let everyone down. But she wasn't here to talk about basketball. One problem at a time. She glanced past Emma as Axel peered into the back of the robot.

"I know. I'm sorry. Look, can I help you guys?"

"We don't need your help," Emma's eyes narrowed. "You think you're so special you can just flounce in and be some big hero. You always think you're so perfect. Well, we can fix this just as well as you can. You don't even know anything about this robot."

Ivy wanted to confess, but couldn't. Emma was mad. If Ivy told her she'd sabotaged the robot, Emma would assume the other Renegades had been involved. She'd never believe they didn't know about it. Ivy would get everyone in trouble the way she'd gotten Wren in trouble with Mr. Vincent. And Tyrone was on the student council. Rumors would get back to Benjamin. Then it would be all over the school.

Even though they hadn't done anything, if the rumor got out, it would destroy Amber, Kammie, and especially Wren. Ivy looked at Axel with sympathy. When she'd stolen the election results, everybody found out. The whole school had turned against her. Now Ivy knew how easy it was to do something impulsive, without realizing the consequences.

Maybe Axel wasn't her favorite person, but a mistake, even a bad one, didn't make her a bad person. And it didn't make Ivy a bad person either. What mattered was what she did next.

"Axel," Ivy leaned around Emma. "If you let me take a look, I might be able to help. Can I help you?"

"Wait!" Axel didn't even hear Ivy. She grabbed Tyrone's arm and pointed to the robot. "It's this jumper right here!"

Axel fiddled with something Ivy couldn't see and looked back and forth from Tyrone's laptop to the robot. Ivy craned her neck around Emma, who still stood like a sentry glaring at Ivy. Tyrone switched his screen from a schematic to a coding app and pressed a button.

The robot moved its arm.

Axel and Tyrone cheered. Coach Bakes, talking to the librarian, scowled up at them. The coach gave Ivy a thoughtful look, then turned back to her discussion.

"See?" Emma said crisply. "We don't need you."

"Good job, Axel!" Ivy called, then turned back to Emma. "I'm sorry I can't be on the team anymore. It wasn't my choice. But hey, you did score more points during the last game than I did."

Emma paused. "You didn't quit on purpose?"

"Absolutely not," Ivy assured her. "But I did something wrong. And I have to earn my way back."

"Like, your mom grounded you or something?" Emma asked.

"Something like that," it was as close to the truth as Ivy could get without getting anyone else in trouble. "Look, Emma. The Machines are awesome. You're awesome. You're the star player now. And Isabelle just needs some practice. Give her a chance."

Emma softened and turned back to the robot. It's movements weren't quite as smooth as they'd been, but it seemed to be moving again. Ivy headed back to her own table. Now that the robot seemed to be repaired, Ivy hoped they could repair the damage done to their teamwork.

Back at their table, she leaned over their collection of mismatched toys, trying to see some sort of common thread. If they could just get a theme, a focus, it would all make sense. Time to rally the team.

"Alright everybody." Ivy, still standing, smacked her hands flat on the table. "It's the bottom of the ninth and we need to step up to the plate. Let's come out swinging and KNOCK THIS BALL OUT OF THE PARK!"

Three pairs of eyes stared back at her blankly.

"I don't understand what that means," Wren replied.

Kammie leaned over, eyes still attentively on Ivy, and whispered out of the corner of her mouth, "I think it's sports talk. Or business talk. They seem to be the same thing."

Amber leaned towards them from the other side, also keeping her eyes on Ivy with a frozen smile. She whispered to them, "Does anyone know what it means though?"

"I understand each word individually," Wren whispered. "But I think she just threw them together and mixed them up like scrambled word eggs."

Ivy rolled her eyes. "Come on guys, I can totally hear you."

They responded with big, fake smiles.

Ivy chuckled. "Okay, okay. I mean we don't have a lot of time left and need to finish strong so we can show the world how great we are, yeah? How's that."

"Oh!" said Amber, understanding dawning in her eyes.

"Gotcha," nodded Kammie.

"Why didn't you just say that?" Wren agreed.

Ivy laughed. "Maybe a slogan, or a theme could help us. Any ideas?"

"Infinity blocks, wind generators, a secret code flashlight," summarized Amber. "A way to relax, a way to harness the unlimited power of nature, and a way to communicate. Hmmm."

"REBELs Incorporated, Toys with Infinite Possibility," Wren blurted.

Ivy blinked. "That's— that's perfect."

"Brilliant!" gushed Amber. "Love it! You're so brilliant, Wren!"

Wren shrugged. "Sometimes my brain works."

"Your brain always works," Ivy patted her on the back. "It just takes the rest of us a while to catch up sometimes. Dr. Kim talked about how valuable out of the box thinkers are to the success of a company in *Success Plan*. Your superpowers are our secret weapon."

Ivy meant it as praise, and was shocked to see tears spring to Wren's eyes. Before she could even ask what was wrong, Wren's face grew determined. She took a deep breath, looked around to see if anyone else could hear, and said quietly, "You guys remember about the extra testing? Well it wasn't just Trixie. I have something I need to tell you."

29

SURPRISE!

"I actually have two things to tell you," Wren corrected herself. "At least two, sort of. I mean, it's not like I counted. But I'm pretty sure I can count to two. Unless there ends up being more that I didn't plan. Things sometimes slip out of my mouth. I always wondered why I babble more than other people. And now I know why."

Wren began to fidget as the others stared at her. All of a sudden she darted under the table.

"Hey, come back," Ivy called. "Don't hide. We're here for you."

"I'm not hiding, I'm getting something." Wren's head popped back over the edge of the table. "For you."

"Oh." Ivy tilted her head. "What is it?"

"I've been trying to do this thing," Wren fiddled with something in her lap. "Sorry it took so long, but I couldn't.

And then you kept asking me questions, but I finally could, so PHEW! Here."

She slid a slightly beat-up book across the table to Ivy. It was her own copy of *Success Plan*, the one she'd loaned to Wren. It wasn't gone forever after all. A wave of relief washed over Ivy as Wren kept talking.

"See, she didn't come until yesterday and I had to wait for that. And I'm sorry I didn't actually read it all. I tried to, I really did." Wren shrugged. "But, see, it's really boring. I mean really, would it have killed her to add a dragon somewhere?"

Ivy ran her hand over the cover. "It's a book about creating a successful future for yourself and your business. Not a lot of context for a dragon. Thanks for returning it, though."

Ivy began to slip the book into her backpack but Wren waved her hands around frantically. Ivy squinted at the erratic movements. Wren's hands flapped and flopped in a mystifying series of motions. Finally, realizing she wasn't communicating clearly, Wren tried adding actual words.

"No, Ivy, wait. There's more. Open it."

Ivy opened the book to the front page.

Words in elegant blue script read, "Ivy, you're an inspiration to your friends. I wish you all the best success. Sincerely, Dr. Caroline Kim."

Ivy almost dropped the book.

She looked from Wren, to the book, to Wren again. Then back to the book. Wren hadn't lost the book at all.

She'd been saving it for Caroline's school visit, to get it autographed.

Wren had slipped away from Mr. Vincent at the presentation, risked getting in trouble, fought her way through crowds of kids despite the noise level, avoided all the other teachers, managed to get Caroline's attention, and even remembered to bring a pen. And, most amazingly for Wren, had managed to keep it all a secret.

For her. For Ivy.

Ivy hugged the book to her chest, fighting back tears. "I don't know what to say. Thank you! This is—oh Wren, thank you."

Wren's face lit up with a wide smile. Amber reached out for the book and Ivy handed it to her. Kammie read Caroline's note over Amber's shoulder with her.

"It's true, you know. You are an inspiration," Kammie said. "You're pretty special, Ivy Rose Park."

Ivy wiped her eyes. "No, no I'm not. If you knew what I've done, you wouldn't be so proud of me. I don't deserve to inspire anybody."

Behind them, Emma stormed out of the library, Tyrone close behind her. Ivy looked over at Axel, sitting alone, glaring after her teammates. Axel was trying so hard to get past her own mistakes. She turned back to the robot and poked at it with a sad finger. Maybe she didn't want to be on the front page of the paper because she was annoying and selfish and wanted lots of attention. Maybe she just wanted people to like her again. Ivy's own mistake hadn't made it any easier for her. When the robot stopped working, Axel's whole group had slipped away one by one. She didn't have the kinds of friends behind her that Ivy did. Friends that came together when things weren't going well, who worked with each other to solve problems.

Friends that deserved the truth.

Ivy needed to tell her friends what she'd done. The spying, the sabotage, getting kicked off the team. Everything she'd been hiding, no matter how embarrassing. They deserved to know.

"I've done something—"

"Wait. I'm not finished," Wren interrupted. "It's still my turn. If I don't tell you guys now, I might never be brave enough. So, the testing. I want to tell you why I had to take more tests."

Ivy clamped her mouth shut. Amber and Kammie looked up from Ivy's book. All eyes turned to Wren. She twisted her hands together while everyone stared and looked away.

"What is it?" Amber asked softly.

"So I'm kind of... I mean," Wren took a deep breath. "Apparently, I'm broken."

Ivy started to say something but Wren held up a hand.

"I have ADHD. And they want to do more tests for a ton of other things like depression, anxiety, autism, and I don't know, a bunch of other stuff. I kind of stopped listening by then." Words poured out of Wren like water over a broken dam. "They also said I'm gifted, whatever that means. Mom says it means I'm smart, but how can I be smart and have ADHD at the same time? And if I'm super smart, wouldn't that mean everything's supposed to be easy? Nothing is easy. My grades are just average, I get in trouble in class and can't concentrate. None of it makes any sense."

Wren grabbed two of the Infinity Blocks and started clicking them together and pulling them apart over and over again. No one said anything.

"Maybe my brain is just too broken to understand," she continued. "I thought maybe I'd have this bright future as a mechanical engineer. Or like Ivy's book, I could make myself a success plan."

She tossed the blocks down with a snarl.

"But I couldn't even read Ivy's book. It was like there was a cat sitting on my head pushing my eyelids closed every time the book got boring. And it was really boring. Sorry Ivy, but it really was. All these other stupid tests are going to tell me what else is wrong with my stupid broken brain and now I probably don't have any future at all."

Silence. Ivy tried to remember what she'd heard about ADHD. It wasn't much, just mostly about rowdy boys who couldn't sit still. That wasn't Wren.

"Do girls even get ADHD?" Ivy asked.

Wren shrugged. "Apparently."

"Are you sure?" Ivy tried to wrap her head around the idea. "Don't worry about it, they probably just messed up."

Wren cringed.

"Maybe it's all just a mistake," Ivy pressed, trying to be supportive.

"I don't think so." Wren squirmed uncomfortably.

"And what if it's not a mistake? Does it have to be a mistake for you to still like me?"

Ivy blinked. She'd been trying to make Wren feel better, but could see how she could have taken it wrong.

"No matter what, it's okay," Amber said softly, sending a warning look to Ivy. "You're the same person you were last week. You just know more about yourself now."

"Right," Ivy tried again to say something supportive, "And you don't have to listen to anybody. You want to be a mechanical engineer, you just put in the work and be the best darn engineer you can be. You're in control of your life. You make your own choices."

It's what her mom would have told Ivy. The sort of supportive words that would make Ivy feel strong, light her competitive fire. But it didn't seem to have the same effect on Wren, who sagged in her chair like the mere words were physically heavy.

"It's not that easy. My brain is a slippery eel. It slides right out of my hands when I try to force it to do something. Or maybe it's like an elephant. I can push it all I want but it's not going anywhere it doesn't want to go."

Ivy leaned forward, trying to understand. "I'm not following you."

"I see, smell, and hear EVERYTHING around me. All the time. I can't shut it out. That's not my choice. I would never choose to never have a break from my senses being overloaded, or from my brain never stopping. Those are things I have to live with, every hour of every day, everywhere I go. I don't get a choice. I just get to try to not fail at everything. Putting in the work means something different to me. I put in the work just to show up every day. It's not about making choices. It's easy for you to make choices."

Ivy looked over at Axel again. "Choices are never easy. Not for anyone."

The table was quiet. Ivy's confession would have to wait. The Expo would have to wait. Wren was the only important thing right now. But Ivy didn't know how to help. She faced problems head-on, with action and confidence. That didn't seem like the best strategy here.

Everything Ivy said only made things worse. Was this how Wren felt? Like every choice was wrong no matter which one she picked? No wonder Wren had trouble just getting through the day sometimes.

"What's it like?" Kammie asked.

"I dunno," Wren shrugged. "What's it like to be anybody? Sometimes I can't stop thinking about stuff, and other times I can't make myself think about anything at all. Sometimes I read the same paragraph in a book fifteen times and still don't know what it says. Sometimes I forget what someone started out saying by the time they finish talking. And then sometimes I forget people are talking WHILE they're talking, and accidentally interrupt them. And everybody yells at me or corrects me all the time, and never just lets me do what I'm doing, which isn't always wrong. Sometimes I just get to the same place by taking a different path but instead of waiting to see where I'm going, people just keep pushing me to their own path. And then when I try to explain that I'm taking my own path or why I'm doing it, they say I'm arguing with them and then everybody starts yelling."

Wren kept talking faster and faster, like the words had been locked inside for a long time. Once the words tasted freedom, they didn't want to stop.

"The testing people said that when other people listen to a teacher or someone talking, they can sort of ignore all the other noises and the colors and lights and all the interesting things in the room. Is that true? I can't even imagine that. I knew in my heart that my brain worked differently than other people's, but no one, not even Principal Sophie, would ever believe me. Just like you Ivy, they just told me I had to try harder, that I was broken at being normal. Not that I was doing a good job at being me. No matter what I do."

"That sounds hard," Kammie replied.

"Yeah," Wren snorted. "I mean, it's not all the time. I'm like a cat getting a bath. I'm perfectly fine sitting in a sunbeam, even though I'm probably totally stinky and need a bath. But oh boy, it's not a good idea to put me in that water. Nope. That's when the trouble starts. I'm both a good kitty and a scratching wet terror with my fur plastered all over my body at the same time."

Wren threw her hands up and stuck out her tongue, pretending to be a cat being forced into the water. She struggled against invisible hands, then pretended to get wet, glaring at them all with an evil expression and a growl. She lifted her hands like claws.

Amber laughed. Then Kammie and Ivy joined in.

Wren chuckled and pulled a few infinity cubes in front of her. She snapped and unsnapped them, redesigning the path over and over again.

"My brain does everything at the same time. How did you explain it, Ivy?" Wren twisted a block. "The circuit that goes in a line like fairy lights and if one part of it burns out, everything stops working?"

"A series circuit?" Ivy asked.

"Yeah, that. I guess most people's brains think thoughts in a row, one leads to another," Wren nodded. "But my brain isn't a series circuit. It's more like the other one—"

"Parallel."

"Yeah, like a parallel circuit. One thought can lead to twenty and each one is just as important as the other. That's how I think, FULL POWER with everything at the same time, or nothing at all."

Wren rotated four T shapes to the top of her blocks, and snapped them together with all four lower stems pointing to one side. Then she took more blocks and snapped them together to create one line that went from one point to another continuously.

"Like this. Imagine there's a light on each block, and that light was an idea, a thought. This one is a parallel brain circuit, with my thoughts sticking out to the side, all sucking power from the main path here at the same time. And this one over here is a series brain circuit. It goes from one thought to the other in a line. That's how it works, right Ivy?"

The Renegade Success Plan

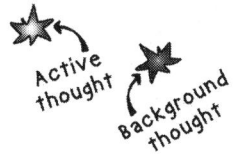  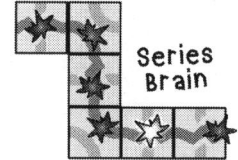

"That's absolutely right." Ivy stared at the blocks in amazement. "You really were listening."

"You're a good teacher," Wren shrugged. "You know, these Infinity paths look like a circuit, like on the motherboard of a computer. Too bad we can't make the blocks electric, huh?"

Wren's casual thought ignited a blinding shower of ideas in Ivy's head. The white electrical energy that had been quiet for weeks now suddenly exploded to life. That was it. Make the blocks electric. "That's brilliant! You're BRILLIANT!"

Ivy visualized the white glow of electricity racing along the Infinity Block paths, twisting and turning. She imagined positive and negative ports attached to the wind generator, powering the blocks, lights on the blocks lighting up when they were put together in a proper circuit. The possibilities were as endless as the paths on the blocks.

If a circuit was an unbroken path out to the thing you were powering and back to the power source, why couldn't that path be made from these blocks? Like train tracks strung together, a straight piece here, a curved one there, to make whatever kind of path you wanted. A puzzle, a game. A toy. You'd have to build the circuit correctly without any breaks or shorts.

Wren, not aware of Ivy's thoughts, collapsed her head onto her folded arms. "It was just a thought."

"No, it's amazing!" Ivy grabbed Wren and pulled her into a hug. "You're amazing."

"Really? I did something right?" Wren's muffled voice came from Ivy's shoulder, her face squished against the taller girl. "Your hoodie is surprisingly tasty, but can you let go?"

"You did something VERY right." Ivy laughed as pulled Wren away and shook her gently by the shoulders. "Your different way of thinking just solved everything."

30

TEAMWORK

"Look here," Ivy traced a path. "We could run wire along here—hmm, no, not a wire. Wires are thick. If we run wires along the paths, they'll come in between the sides of the blocks and keep them from touching. Then the magnets won't touch either and won't hold the blocks together. We need these blocks to click together and stay there. Maybe we can put the wires on the inside?"

"What about this? Can we use it as the light we'd be powering?" Kammie held up the code thrower. "I know it's not a block, but could it be some kind of a plug-in accessory?"

"Good idea," Ivy replied. "As long as there's a way to attach the accessory to the positive and negative sides of your circuit, it should work. At least in theory. We just need to make sure there's enough power."

"Can we use the windmill to supply the power?"

Amber turned the blades. "I know we didn't get it hooked up to make actual electricity yet, but maybe we can figure it out."

"Well, if we could get it working, it would just need a positive and negative wire to connect to the block circuit, like the accessories." Ivy considered it. "The blocks would be the path. But how to stick the wires to the blocks? Oh! What about magnets? If we could wrap the stripped wire parts around magnets, they would snap to the block magnets and hold the wire to the path."

"So are some of the blocks going to do things when the circuit is complete, too? Like light up or buzz?" Wren asked.

"Great idea. In electronics they call the thing you're powering a 'load.' so the light or the buzzer would be the circuit's load, whether it was on a block or attached like an accessory." Ivy squeezed the code thrower and it lit up. She pointed to the LED light. "Here, the LED is the load, the battery is the power supply, and the wires are the conductive path. So that's our simple circuit."

"So we just need to make sure our circuit blocks have those parts in order for them to be a simple circuit too, right?" Amber asked. "The wind generator is the power supply, the accessory or the lights on the blocks are the load, and the path is the conductive path, right?"

"Yup," Ivy nodded. "Our jobs here are to get the wind generator generating and rig it up with a positive and negative wire, get the code thrower rigged up with a positive and negative wire too instead of the battery, and make the paths conductive. Wow, we might actually be able to do this."

Wren spun the blade on the wind generator. "I can see if I can figure out how to generate power with this thing."

"Sounds good, you're our best creative thinker, and that's a creative job," Ivy agreed. "Amber, you and I can use our experience from making the light-up purse to work on making the blocks conductive."

"That leaves converting this thing to me." Kammie looked at the code thrower skeptically. "I still don't really understand how all this electricity stuff works, but I can try."

Ivy patted her shoulder. "Give it a shot. You'll get it."

Wren disappeared into the book stacks to research while Kammie squinted at the code thrower. She grabbed some scrap paper, drawing some ideas. The hush of focus descended on their table while teams in the rest of the library argued and frantically filled out paperwork.

Ivy glanced around. "If we can pull this off, we still might have a chance at winning."

"I keep telling you this isn't a competition," Amber shook her head. "We've already made a perfectly good company. This new idea? I'm in it because it's fun. That's all that matters now."

Ivy didn't say anything. She squinted at the block in her hand. What did they need to create a path for the electricity? Usually, wire was the best solution. A wire's metal core conducted electricity really well, which meant it could move easily through it, like running on a flat, clean track. A rubber coating surrounded the metal wire like a jacket. Rubber insulated the wire, which meant the electricity couldn't move easily through the wire, like surrounding your running track with deep pits of sand and walls of bushes. You could get through it if you tried hard enough, but mostly you'd stay on the nice easy track. But wire wouldn't work. They needed something thin and flat so the blocks would still link together.

"What about the conductive thread?" Ivy asked. "We could sew it, or even tape it along the path."

"We do have some left," Amber considered. "But wouldn't it be too thin? How could you make sure the threads touched each other? And wouldn't tape insulate the thread anyway?"

"You're absolutely right," Ivy agreed. "But I can't think of anything that's flat, metal, and doesn't have to be taped."

She tapped the block against the table. Suddenly, Amber's eyes lit up.

"I know! Copper tape!"

"Copper tape?" Ivy stared at her. "Is that a thing? It sounds perfect."

"Yes, the tape I use in my garden." Amber glowed. "It's metal and flat, and sticks like a sticker! You said copper is one of the best conductors. And it looks nice too. But would we have to cover all the paths with it? Their colors are so pretty."

"Actually that's a really good point, for more than just the colors." Ivy followed the path around and around again. "If we make all these paths copper, they'll all connect together and the circuit will short out."

"So we just choose certain paths to copperize." Amber shrugged. "Would that work?"

"If we're careful. We just need to make sure the copper on the conductive path parts goes all the way down to the magnets on at least two of its sides so everything will connect."

"Two?" Amber asked.

"Yeah, an input and an output. A place for the path to go in and out. We can add an LED in the middle of some of the paths we copperize, so you can see when your circuit works, even if you don't hook it up to an accessory. It would be really fun!"

Amber frowned. "But LED lights are big lumps. They'd keep the blocks from connecting to each other, right?"

"True," Ivy admitted. "But it's only some of the blocks. And it's just a prototype. We could make all kinds of blocks, like resistors, and capacitors—"

Amber laughed. "Let's not go crazy. Don't forget we don't have much time."

Ivy sighed. They were coming up with so many great ideas, she hated to lose them. "Maybe we can just write it all down for later."

"What do you mean?" Kammie's head popped up. She

pushed the code thrower away from her with a sour look. "I can't figure this out."

Kammie was smart, but Ivy knew converting the code thrower didn't use her strengths. She could tell Kammie was getting frustrated and starting to feel like a failure when in reality, the task just wasn't the right one for her.

But you know what she was good at? Lists. Reports. Organizing information. It was her strength, and it was just what they needed to move them forward.

"How about you figure out a way to list and present all the ideas we have that we don't have time to actually complete right now?" Ivy suggested.

"Oh!" Kammie began taking notes furiously, and somehow, still legibly. "I can totally do that. I can collate everything, you know, gather up all the different ideas and organize them. Present where our company came from, where it is now, and where we want to take it in the future. Linear progression is my specialty."

Kammie happily began listing all the different ideas they'd thrown out like she did when they brainstormed. Ivy felt a huge weight being lifted from her. With someone like Kammie at the wheel, the future of their company was in good, well organized hands.

Ivy turned back to the infinity circuit blocks, contemplating copper tape. From the corner of her eye she saw a shape moving towards them from the book stacks.

"Look! Looklookloookity. Look what I found!" Wren dropped a book on the table and pointed to a painting of a man on the cover. "This guy was named Michael Faraday and he had funny hair. He invented the world's first electrical generator after a whole bunch of experiments with magnets and stuff. His brains transformed the entire way people live forever. But guess what?"

"What?" Amber asked.

"He had ADHD, too." Wren looked at them with glittering eyes. "This guy was a total genius. It makes me think that, I dunno, maybe I have a future after all. Maybe just because I think different, it doesn't mean I'm dumb or broken. Maybe I'm just different."

Ivy watched Wren's face glow with the promise of her own potential power. She truly was a powerhouse. A pinch hitter. She just walked a different path.

"You know the thing about parallel and series circuits?" Ivy said. "Neither one is better than the other, they just do different jobs. A series circuit takes less wire and less effort to build, and it's easier to troubleshoot, but if one part of it breaks, the whole thing goes down. In a parallel circuit, each component works independently, so if one goes out the others still work. But it takes more power and can overheat. Everything has strengths and weaknesses."

Without everyone working together, they'd just have a bunch of disconnected ideas. Ivy used to think her friends were full of potential, they just needed help to get there. But they didn't need help. They just needed to do what they did best. All their strengths working together would make them one of the best companies at the Expo.

"You just have to know which connection to use." Ivy

pushed both block circuit examples Wren had made to the center of the table. "They're both equally important. They're both essential."

CIRCUIT

MATERIALS
- Infinity blocks or template
- Copper tape
  (with conductive adhesive)
- Battery holder and batteries
- LEDs
- Small, powerful magnets
  (Keep away from little kids!!)
- Scissors and Markers as needed

If needed, construct Infinity Blocks according earlier instructions. Asse them before or after ad the circuit components

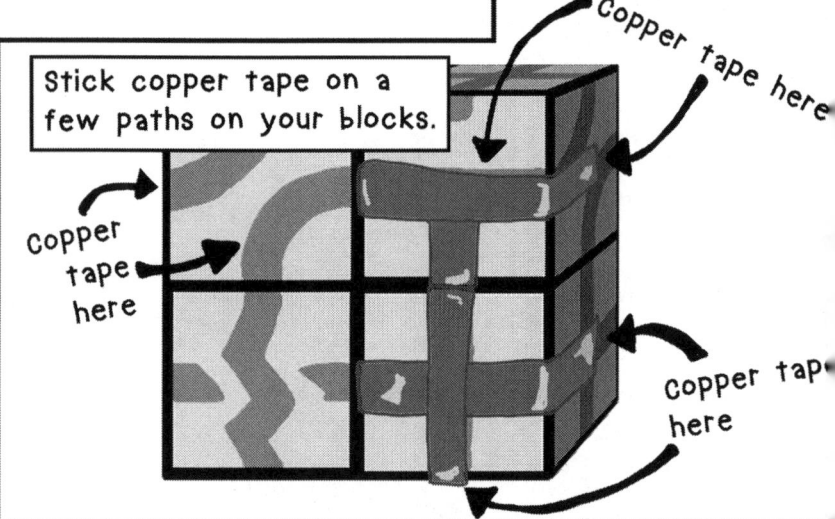

Stick copper tape on a few paths on your blocks.

Copper tape here
Copper tape here
Copper tape here

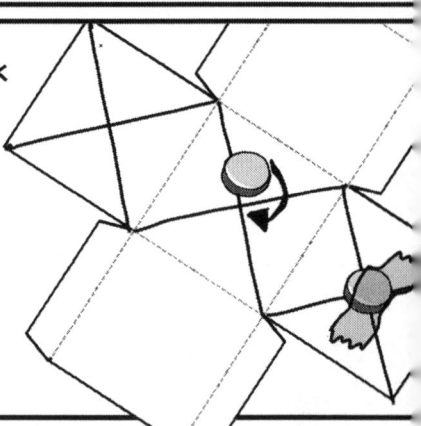

Tape a magnet to the back of each face.

Find center by connecting the corners in an X.

Tape the magnet at the center of the X.

BLOCKS

d LEDs to a few blocks between
o unconnected paths.

Copper tape is hard to work with! Don't get discouraged!

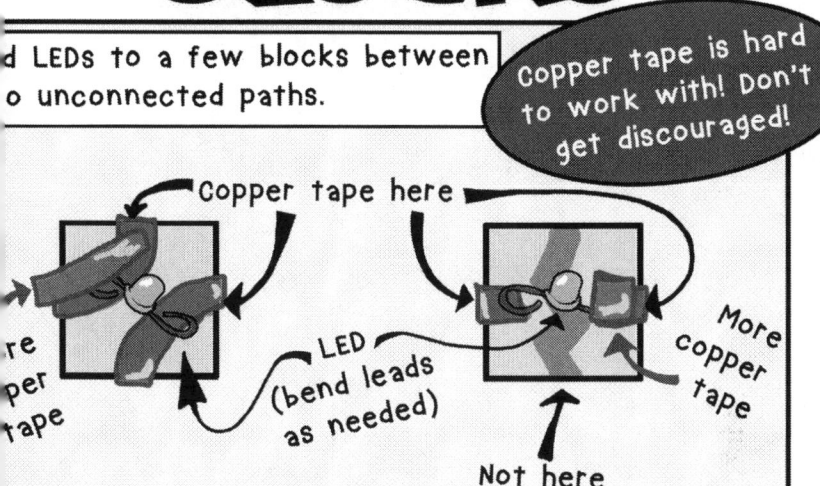

Copper tape here

re
per
tape

LED (bend leads as needed)

More copper tape

Not here

Secure lead by sandwiching it between copper path and more copper tape on top.

PS

hesive MUST
conductive!

e copper
uld cover
magnets on
sides.

nit the
hs you put
per on, to
e it easier
create a
king circuit.

Wrap the raw ends of each wire coming from the batter pack around a magnet, and secure with copper tape. DO NOT LET THESE MAGNETS STICK TO EACH OTHER- Keep positive and negative leads separate.

31

CONVERSION

"Do you think we'll be able to make the wind generator make actual electricity?" Kammie sorted through her notes. "That seems like a lot of work."

"I found some ideas that would work, but we'd need special tools, and a lot more time than we have," Wren admitted. "I don't think we'll get it done in time."

If the four of them really pushed, if they stayed up all night and ignored their other responsibilities, maybe. They'd have to put off homework and spend every possible moment in the library. They'd have a spectacular night at the Expo, maybe they'd get on the front page of the paper again. And then they'd go home.

Would any of it matter on Monday morning?

Kids all over the library rushed to get the last touches on their projects. A groan came from Axel's table as their robot toppled over. It was working, but not as well as it had been. Was it the code, or was it still not fixed from what

Ivy had done? If Ivy could only get Axel and Emma to let her take a look at the robot, she would know. But she didn't see a way to get to them with all the other kids around.

Kids.

The Entrepreneurial Expo was a great way for kids to learn about business like the ones experienced adults like Caroline spent years developing.

They were just kids. Sixth grade. Ivy sometimes forgot that.

It was important to do a good job, but not everything needed one thousand percent effort. Some things could just be good enough once in a while. Especially when "good enough" was actually really, really good.

Ivy thought about Amber's mother, worrying so much about keeping people happy that she didn't have fun at her own son's party. It was a great party. An accomplishment to be proud of. Maybe Amber's mom enjoyed all the work. But maybe she just wanted to dance, the way Wren had talked Ivy into dancing. To set things aside for a while and just enjoy.

Ivy's own mom popped into her thoughts. Ivy respected her so much. She'd worked so hard to be successful in an industry where it wasn't easy to be a mom at all, much less a single mom. And she still made time to give Ivy everything she needed. But her mom didn't always make time for herself. To give herself what she needed, too.

Some things were worth that kind of sacrifice, Ivy thought. Meeting Caroline was worth that kind of sacrifice. But not to the rest of the team. And maybe they were right.

Sometimes it was okay to just do what you could do, and let that be enough, whether it impressed Dr. Caroline Kim or not, even if you really, really hoped it did.

Ivy shook her head. "I don't think we can. But we do need some way to get power to these blocks if we're going to convert them. To be able to show how they work. Any ideas?"

"Cheat!" Wren exclaimed. "We can cheat!"

Ivy gasped. "What?"

"Hide a battery pack in the windmill," Wren grinned. "We can pull the red and black wires out and use those, right? It's not really cheating as long as you tell people you're doing it though."

Battery packs were made to provide electricity to circuits. It was a great idea. They could just use technology that already existed. All technology was built on other technology, after all. Science wouldn't get very far if people just reinvented the same things over and over.

"Excellent," agreed Ivy. "Let's cheat."

And this time, she didn't even have to feel bad about it.

32

THE ENTREPRENEURIAL EXPO

"Do you have everything you need, honey?" Ivy's mom asked as they climbed into the car Friday afternoon.

"I think I'm good." Everything was at school, in their cubby. Her mom had taken the whole evening off to go to the Expo, just to be with Ivy. To support her. To have fun.

They were the first Renegades to arrive. Ivy and her mom pulled everything out of their cubby. They brought paperwork, a shoebox full of Infinity Circuit Blocks, and the wind generator with the battery pack tucked inside.

The cubes weren't perfect, but with a proper circuit path and a little push, the electricity could travel from the batteries to light up the LEDs on a block, or even the code thrower Ivy had managed to convert. It hadn't been hard, just pulling the wires off the battery and wrapping them around magnets then taping them down with some copper tape.

None of it worked flawlessly, but it all worked. And Kammie's "production plan" paperwork included diagrams and explanations and new ideas. A theoretical future for the company.

As Ivy led her mom to the gym, Wren ran up, almost tackling her.

"You're early," Ivy smiled at her. "Nice job."

"I know, right?!" Wren grinned. "Mom is trying this new idea where she creates routines. It seemed a little silly at first but, hey, hard to argue with success."

Wren fell into step next to Ivy. She even waved to Bobby as he waited at the crosswalk between the school and the gym. To Ivy's surprise, Bobby waved back.

Kids streamed into the gym, carrying poster board and boxes filled with their business supplies. Benjamin stood at the door to the gym holding a clipboard. He waved to Ivy and Wren as they approached.

"Hello, mighty Renegades! Or I should say Mighty REBELs," He glanced down at the clipboard. "Oh. Your table is all the way in the back. Table G3. That's the third aisle and, well, all the way against the wall."

He looked up apologetically.

"Sounds great," Ivy replied. "That'll be just fine."

"You're not going to get quite as much traffic back there," Benjamin shrugged. Then he shared a glowing smile with them. "This event has really been the highlight of Career Week. Thanks for the idea, Wren. I appreciate you all helping me make this week into everything I'd hoped. All our hard work paid off, I think kids will remember this one for a long time."

"Thanks! And you're welcome," Wren glowed back at him. "People will be talking about it for years. Also, if you see that guest speaker, Caroline Kim, you tell her to stop by our table no matter how out of the way it is. You should come by too, we made something fantastic."

"I would expect nothing less," he laughed, then pointed to a perky blond ponytail ahead of them. "Just follow Axel Andrews. She's table 3B. She snagged some prime real estate!"

As Benjamin turned to welcome the team behind them, Ivy added, "Hey, you did a great job. This whole week has been amazing, Benjamin. The school will never forget you."

Benjamin paused. He met her gaze. Ivy was surprised to see the vulnerability in his eyes. She'd always thought Benjamin was fearless with unerring confidence. A flawlessly efficient circuit. But there, in his deep brown eyes, she could see his doubt. He wasn't a circuit at all. He was just a boy, trying to be good enough.

He blinked a few times rapidly, as if something was in his eye, and gave her a soundless, grateful nod. Then he looked away quickly.

"Thanks, Ivy." He coughed to clear his throat. "I really hope so. I just—"

"Yeah," Ivy laid a hand on his arm. "I know what you mean. It can be hard to live up to expectations."

Then she led the way into the crowd.

Axel, Emma, Tyrone and the others in their group taped a giant banner proclaiming "CODERVILLE" to their table. They didn't seem excited. Axel balanced the beautiful white robot on the table as they passed. Tyrone synced his laptop to it and began to run it through its paces. No one smiled.

"It's good enough," Emma said, leaning back in a folding chair.

"No," Axel snipped. "It has to be perfect. Don't you understand how important this is?"

Ivy felt her enthusiasm fade as Axel's desperate voice disappeared behind her. Sometimes things could be good enough. And sometimes they needed to be more. This Expo was important to Axel. Just like Benjamin, she had a lot more wrapped up in this event than the other participants. Maybe she was lonely. Maybe she had something to prove. And Ivy had made it harder. She'd have to confess to her friends, but the difference between Ivy's friends and Axel's was that she knew the Renegades wouldn't abandon her when they learned the truth. Even if the whole school found out. Most people didn't have friends like that.

Axel didn't have friends like that.

Ivy pledged to herself to make her own part in their problems right. It was possible that any remaining issues with the robot were in their code, but just in case it was something with the wiring, something Ivy had done, she had to fix it. She owed it to them.

They reached table G3 and began to set up.

"Ivy, honey," her mom rotated a block and snapped it

to another one. "These are great. I can't believe you girls made them!"

A squeal got their attention. Amber thundered down the aisle, dancing gracefully out of the way of the growing crowd to plow into Wren with a giant hug. She pulled a long piece of butcher paper out of her bag.

"I made us a sign!" Amber gushed, unrolling the paper. It said *REBELs Incorporated, Toys With Infinite Possibility* in big, colorful letters. And underneath it said *Makers of the Infinity Circuit Blocks*. She taped it to the edge of the table.

It was better than good enough. It was beautiful.

"Has anyone heard from Kammie?" Ivy asked, glancing at the clock on her phone. "It's not like her to be late."

"Total bizarro," Wren agreed. "I'm early, she's late. What is this world coming to?"

"You've done an amazing job, ladies," Ivy's mom said. Then she saw Amber's mom in the crowd and waved to her. "If you don't need me for a little while, I'd like to go look around."

"Sure." Ivy glanced down the aisle at Axel's booth. "I've got some stuff I need to take care of anyway."

Her mom hugged her, then disappeared into the crowd. The gym was getting more and more crowded, and there was still no sign of Kammie. But as Ivy searched for her friend in the crowd, she saw a familiar head making its way along the aisles.

It was Caroline Kim. She'd come as promised. A

familiar yearning blossomed inside Ivy. That hunger. If she could just meet Caroline, all the work, all the sacrifices, even getting kicked off the Lovelace Machines basketball team would be worth it.

Caroline pointed out a route to one of the people with her, pointing up and down the aisles. Then she looked way in the back of the room, where their table was, and pointed along the back row. They'd be one of the last booths she visited. Ivy hoped she wouldn't get bored and leave first.

Ivy also realized that Caroline would be at Axel's booth much sooner. Even though meeting Dr. Kim wasn't a priority for Axel, Ivy still wanted to fix the robot before she got there.

Then, all of a sudden, Amber broke out in the most ear-splitting shriek Ivy had ever heard. Ivy's ears rang above the noise already filling the gym.

"What? What is it?" Ivy looked around frantically. Had someone sat on the blocks? Was there a fire?

No. It was Kammie. And her dad. And her mom.

Who was carrying a little boy.

"YOU'RE HERE!" Amber screamed, then cringed when the boy buried his head in Kammie's mom's shoulder. "Oh, oh, I'm sorry, I don't mean to scare the little guy."

"He's super brave," Kammie beamed at them, holding out a finger to the boy. He reached out immediately and grabbed the finger in one chubby little hand. Their skin was the exact same beautiful brown. "I think he likes all the activity. Guys, meet Batuk. My new brother."

Ivy could hardly see him around Amber, who was

doing an admirable job not pouncing on the poor kid. Batuk looked around the room with wide, wondering eyes, taking in everything. One arm wrapped around Kammie's mother—his mother—and the other clung to Kammie's finger. Kammie's dad, standing behind them, saw the display on the table.

"So this is what you did with all those magnets, Kaminia?" He snapped a few blocks together. "Nice."

"I'm available for babysitting any time, day or night," Amber babbled at Kammie's mom, eyes riveted on Kammie's brother. "Seriously, I'll skip Hebrew class if I need to."

A movement down the aisle caught Ivy's attention. Caroline had finished walking down the first aisle and was heading to the second.

She'd be at Axel's table soon.

"I've got to go take care of something," Ivy told the others.

"What?" cried Wren. "You can't leave now!"

"It's important," Ivy called over her shoulder as she made her way through the crowd. One last mission. This time, for the right reasons. "I'll explain later."

Axel was near tears. Emma yawned and rolled her eyes while Tyrone threw Axel a dirty look every time she made a noise.

"What's up?" Ivy tried to sound casual. "Your booth looks great."

"It's not perfect," Axel gasped between near-hysterical breaths. "I keep trying to make the robot walk and it just wobbles. Half the time it falls down. I don't know what else to try, and Gail is on her way over to interview us for the paper. The paper, Ivy! This is my big chance to finally get on the cover."

"It's fine," Emma grumbled from her chair. Tyrone nodded and typed something on his laptop. "Seriously, it's good enough."

But it wasn't. Not for Axel. If Ivy understood anything, she understood how Axel felt.

"I bet everything will work out," Ivy reassured her. She picked up the robot. No one stopped her.

A noise in the crowd caught everyone's attention. Ivy took the opportunity to flip the robot over and look at its controls. The back panel was still off, leaving the motherboard exposed. Ivy scanned the circuitry for the jumper she'd changed. It was hard to remember, but she was pretty sure she found the right one. And sure enough, it wasn't in the same position it had been in originally.

It was hard to focus with everything going on, but Ivy knew just what to do.

33

COLLAPSE

Fixing the glitch took longer than Ivy thought it would. There were a few other little changes they'd made trying to accommodate her sabotage. Ivy had to put everything back to the way it had been originally.

She made her final tweak, and set the robot down again. Axel and her team hadn't even noticed she was doing anything more than looking at it.

"Can you show me something?" Ivy asked.

"I can try," Axel pressed a key on Tyrone's laptop with a shaking hand.

The robot walked forward. Steady, balanced. Perfect.

Axel cheered. "Oh Ivy! You're like tech support! You just stand next to the computer and it starts working again."

Ivy forced herself to laugh. "Your code looks solid, nice work. You guys should be proud."

With a wave, Ivy headed back to her own booth. She

should still have plenty of time to get back and practice what she'd say a few times just in case Caroline did come by. There was plenty of time to wait if Caroline stuck with her pattern.

As she pushed towards her booth, Ivy closed her eyes, just for a second, to imagine what it might feel like to shake Caroline's hand. She had so many things she wanted to tell her. She could tell her how much she respected her amazing work as an electrical engineer, how wonderful her inventions were, how she hoped to work at one of Caroline's companies one day, and how much she enjoyed the book. She could still ask her if she'd be her mentor. It was a dream, but Ivy was allowed to dream.

She opened her eyes—and froze.

Caroline Kim was walking away from Ivy's booth.

The familiar head bobbed above the crowd of parents and students between them. She had visited the table while Ivy was gone. She'd broken her pattern.

Ivy wasn't back yet, and Caroline was walking away.

Ivy panicked.

"Wait!" She yelled. Several people turned to stare at her, but Ivy didn't care. She began to run, pushing her way through the crowd. Ivy called again.

Caroline couldn't hear her. She headed towards Axel's booth as the surge of people swallowed her. And just like that, Caroline disappeared down aisle two. Ivy imagined she'd wrap back up aisle three, missing the back wall entirely on the new pass.

And Ivy hadn't even had the chance to say hi.

Maybe she could still reach her in time. Ivy pushed frantically through the crowd of people, desperate. If she could just reach the booth, maybe Caroline would turn back. Maybe she forgot something and would come back. Maybe—

Ivy finally made it to her booth, eyes never leaving the dark head that got smaller and smaller as it moved away. Far out of reach.

She wasn't coming back.

Ivy turned frantic eyes to the Renegades. Amber and Kammie chatted happily over Batuk's small, alert head, oblivious. Amber had somehow convinced Mrs. Doyle to let her hold him, and Amber looked like she was in heaven.

Wren, however, saw Ivy. Her smile almost swallowed her whole face.

"Ivy!" Wren gushed. "You just missed Doctor Kim! She was really nice. And she loved the Infinity Circuit Blocks. We had a big long chat with her, all of us! I wish you'd have been here. She was asking about you. Where did you go?"

Everything hit Ivy all at once. Her bad choices, getting thrown off the basketball team, Wren's diagnosis, Kammie's new brother, everything had changed so quickly, so dramatically. She hadn't had time to just pause and get used to any of it. And now the success plan she'd set up so carefully had shorted out like a bad circuit, exploding in her face.

She sank to her knees, then sat on the floor. She knew she'd messed things up, but she was trying to learn.

Couldn't she just have this one thing? Couldn't she at least tell Caroline that she'd made a difference in Ivy's life?

Apparently not. Apparently, her bad choice had cost her everything. Ivy covered her face with her hands, and for the first time in years, began to cry.

She'd tried to do the right thing, learned so much, but still had to pay the price of her decisions. She'd lost her chance to be part of the winning basketball team. And now she'd lost the only chance she'd ever have to meet the one person she really wanted to meet. It was what she deserved.

Ivy glanced back at Axel's booth. There was Caroline. Watching the team run their robot through its programmed paces. It worked perfectly. Caroline reached out to shake Axel's hand. A light flashed as Gail took a picture of Caroline and Axel's handshake.

Axel would get her front page photo after all.

After all her hard work, it was what she deserved, too. Axel didn't need to be punished for her bad choice any more. But now it was Ivy's turn. She just hoped some day she would earn her way back.

"Ivy," Wren shook her shoulder.

Ivy pulled away and cried harder. It was embarrassing. Her mom would be back any minute. A few people walking by looked over at her in the corner, sobbing like a baby. Worse than a baby. The only baby nearby was in Amber's arms, and he wasn't crying at all. Ivy had brought it all on herself. She shouldn't have left the booth.

Coderville's robot was doing fine. They would have been good enough.

And yet—

No, Ivy didn't regret fixing the robot. If she lost, it was a fair loss. She could hold her head up and know that she'd done her best to do the right thing. She'd fixed her mistake.

And that was worth the heartache.

"Ivy," Wren held something out to her. "I've been trying to tell you. Here."

It took a minute for Ivy to comprehend what Wren held out to her. She reached for it without thinking. It was a small, rectangular piece of thick cardstock.

The name Dr Caroline Kim, along with the logo of Sapai Industries, was printed on it. Along with her private email address. Ivy wiped her eyes, trying to understand what she held.

Confused, she turned it over.

Printed neatly on the other side in blue ink were the words "To the girl in the photo. I'll see you soon."

"She wants to meet you, Ivy," Wren nodded. "She's coming back at the end of the show."

Ivy turned the business card over in her hand, not quite believing what she was seeing. Why would Caroline give her her own personal business card?

"But why?" she asked out loud.

Wren shrugged. "I don't know, but she said specifically that she wants to meet you."

34

IT'S NOT ABOUT THE THING

The Expo was almost over by the time Caroline returned to their booth.

Kammie and her family left early to put Batuk to bed. Her whole family looked exhausted. Ivy was honestly impressed they'd all made it at all, but Kammie would never abandon them. And her family would never abandon Kammie.

Wren and Amber had taken turns walking about the Expo, checking out the other tables, chatting with the other entrepreneurs, learning more about everyone's businesses. They went together to find Milo's table, even further tucked away than their own booth. Everyone else explored the Expo from top to bottom.

But Ivy waited.

By the time Caroline returned, the crowd in the gym had thinned considerably. Some kids were already pulling down their displays and packing up their merchandise.

Axel also spent the whole Expo at her booth, radiant in her success. Ivy could see her whenever there was an opening in the crowds. Axel shone as she talked to visitors, running them through her business plan while Emma or Tyrone showed off the robot's code. Not many people made it all the way back to the REBELs' booth, but there was only one Ivy cared about.

"Ah," Caroline called in a clear, strong voice as she approached. "There you are. The girl who invited me here. The one in the photo. Thanks for contacting me, I'm impressed with your school's whole Career Week. That student council president of yours is quite the force of nature."

"Oh, yes, Benjamin. Yes. Benjamin. Force of nature." Words fell from Ivy's mouth unfiltered until she managed to take a deep breath. That was no way to make a good impression. "It's a pleasure to meet you in person."

THE Dr. Caroline Kim finally stood in front of her. Ivy extended her hand, like she had a thousand times in her imagination. Part of her thought Caroline might not shake it, even now.

But Caroline reached out and grasped her hand. Her grip was warm and firm, and filled Ivy with energy.

"I'm pleased to meet you as well," Caroline said.

"So," Ivy grasped for something more to say. "Do you want your card back?"

Caroline laughed. "You hold on to that. I don't give those out to just anybody."

"Cool. Thanks. Great. Um hey, so," Caroline had said

to be bold in her book, so Ivy decided to do the boldest thing she'd ever done. "Um, would you consider being my mentor?"

Caroline sized her up. "You're a little too young yet, Ivy. But you look me up in a few years if you're still interested and we'll talk. You have my card."

Ivy nodded. It was more than she could have realistically hoped for. She slid the card into her pocket, careful not to crease it.

"Did Wren give you a good rundown on REBELs Incorporated?" Ivy asked, trying to prolong the conversation. "We didn't have time to finish, but did you like our product?"

Caroline picked up a block. "Absolutely. Your idea has legs. I can see a product like this doing very well at market. It's fun, attractive, educational, and inventive. I especially like the wind generator. Nice touch."

"I wish we'd had time to make it actually work," Ivy apologized.

"You can't do everything." Caroline laughed again. "I love the fact that you created a roadmap. It shows a real vision for your company's future. No one else at this Expo did anything like that. It's one of the main reasons I think you've done the best job here. You've got a real path to success, Ivy."

"Wren led us most of the way," Ivy confessed. "She's a born leader. We all had important roles, but she's a creative genius."

They both turned to watch the genius at work at the

other end of the table. Wren, oblivious, pulled apart blocks and snapped them together. She stretched her mouth into a giant "O" every time the light turned on, and snapped it shut as the light turned off.

She looked like a goldfish.

"She's, ummm, more than you might expect," Ivy winced.

"Aren't we all?" An amused smile played across Caroline's face.

"You really think these toys would sell well?" Ivy asked.

"I do," Caroline answered. "But that's not what makes your company so good."

"Isn't that the point of a company?" Ivy watched Wren balance a block on her head. "To create something that sells?"

"That may be the point of a company," Caroline replied. "But it's not the point of a leader. A product is not going to make your company successful by itself. A good company isn't only about the thing you're making. It's never been about the thing, Ivy. Not for me. Products come and go. There will always be another thing. A successful company is made of people."

Caroline inclined her head towards Wren, who was now sniffing the blocks.

"The best leader isn't the person who makes the best thing. They're the one with the best team. A company built around a thing is destined to fail eventually. Things don't last forever, especially in technology. The startup world is littered with the corpses of companies that only built themselves around some great new technology. Then something better came along. Unless the company has the ability to pivot, they will die along with the technology. Remember pagers? Probably not, they were dead before you were born."

It was like what Mrs. Mailloux had said. Technology wasn't just about electronics. It was about inventing ways to solve problems. A basketball game wasn't about each game, it was about the season, and beyond that, about the players and the coach. With good players and a good coach you could keep winning season after season.

Caroline continued. "The most successful companies aren't just about one thing, and they don't have just one kind of person on their teams, either. A good team can look at problems from all sides, with people who can draw from all sorts of different life experiences to find unique ways to deal with the problems they're solving. A good leader recognizes the strengths of her team, in whatever forms they come, and helps each person develop those strengths. There are a lot of good ideas out there, but only a few of them will make it to production. Integrity, teamwork, agency, creativity, flexibility. Trust. That's what you want in a business. That comes from the people."

Down the aisle, Axel's robot danced exactly as it was programmed. Emma sat on the sidelines, spinning a pencil around her fingers. She was the only team member of Coderville left except for Axel. Axel had accomplished her goal. Tyrone, Emma and the others would no doubt get the good grades they'd hoped for. But they hadn't built a strong team. Their company would dissolve after tonight and, satisfied, none of them would care.

Then Ivy thought about her own Renegades. How everyone worked together. Wren, with her crazy lightning cloud of ideas and outside-the-box thinking. Amber, taking in everything without judgement, observing and remembering. Kammie, logical, hardworking, organized, and always ready to help. And Ivy herself. Not someone who made good choices and bad choices. Someone who learned, and grew, and fixed problems. Ivy was willing to make hard choices and step up to the plate. She got things done.

"Success is a team sport," Caroline said, as if reading her mind. "You don't lead because someone puts you in a leadership role. You lead because the people on your team want to follow you."

Tomorrow might be the end of REBELs Incorporated, but their team would still be there, stronger than ever. Not because of Infinity Circuit Blocks or unfinished wind generators, and not because of front page photos.

They'd still be there because they were a team. They were the Renegades. They'd chosen to see each other for who they really were, and no bad choice would tear them apart.

"At the end of the day, Ivy, you have to be proud of yourself. If you want a strong team, you have to be worthy of a strong team. Your team," Amber returned to the table and Caroline pointed to her and Wren. "Your team is strong. You know how I know? Because they're proud of themselves. And they're proud of you. You've seen the value of each player on your team. When people feel valued, that's when they do things everyone can be proud of."

Caroline Kim looked Ivy straight in the eyes.

"That's how you have a winning team, Ivy. You lead them."

35

THE END

*I*vy pulled the microscope off the Greenhouse shelf. It seemed like ages since they'd been in their workshop, and even longer since they'd used their precious microscope. It was time to do something fun.

The sun warmed the inside of the Greenhouse as Kammie told Amber and Wren stories about being a new big sister. Amber hung on every word, but Wren rolled her eyes a lot.

"Hey Ivy," Wren interrupted another story about drool. "When you're big and famous working for that Dr. Kim, you can buy us new eyepieces to replace those broken ones."

"If I work for Dr. Kim," Ivy pulled the slides off their shelf. "I'll buy us a whole new microscope."

"You won't," Amber frowned. "That would be wasteful. This one is perfectly good. We just need to fix what's broken."

Ivy laughed. "Of course. But for now, I'm going to investigate the wonders of—" She reached into the box and selected a slide at random. "Dragonfly wings! Oh, nice one."

She fitted the slide into the stage of the microscope and snapped the slide holders over it. Flipping on the backlight, she peered into the regular magnification eyepieces, the ones that still worked. Immediately she was transported into a microscopic realm of wonder. Iridescent, irregular shapes spread out like a stained-glass window. The delicate films between the irregular lines held just enough color to be visible, but still look like gossamer ghosts. Ivy imagined a dragonfly skimming over still water, zipping from moment to moment, with wings vibrating so quickly they blurred.

"You guys, look at this," She offered.

Amber put her eyes against the eyepieces and sighed happily.

"What a great day," Amber said.

Sun poured into Wren's yard. Through the window, Ivy could see Trixie flopped on the grass. She'd started to head to the Greenhouse to join them, but the warm sun had caught her like a cat and now she spread out on her back, arms outstretched.

"Now that we know Trixie is dyslexic," Wren gazed out the window at her sister, "she's going to get some help. I know she'll never be the strongest reader, but I hope she'll at least get some of her confidence back. She's a smart kid,

The Renegade Success Plan

I've actually kind of missed her hanging out with us. Is that weird?"

"I miss her too," Amber agreed.

"I don't know. Little siblings are a big adventure," Kammie added sagely. "And really loud. A lot louder than I expected."

"Guess you're not going to have much spare time anymore, Kammie," Amber pointed out. "All of us are so busy lately. I guess it'll only get worse. That's what Gail and Benjamin say anyway."

Quiet filled the Greenhouse. But it wasn't an awkward kind of quiet. It was a comfortable, familiar quiet. They knew they'd make time for each other. They didn't even have to say it. That's what you did for friends, Ivy thought. You made time.

"Well," Amber broke the silence. "Now that Ivy is off the basketball team and the Expo is over, she, at least, will have a little time to breathe, right?"

"Oh, I don't know," Ivy leaned back and crossed her fingers behind her head. "I hear playing an instrument looks great on your college applications. I enjoyed playing the guitar at the Bar Mitzvah. Now that I have some time, I'll have to look into lessons."

The others laughed.

"Can't you just relax and have some fun?" Wren asked.

"Yeah," Ivy agreed. "Yeah, I think I can."

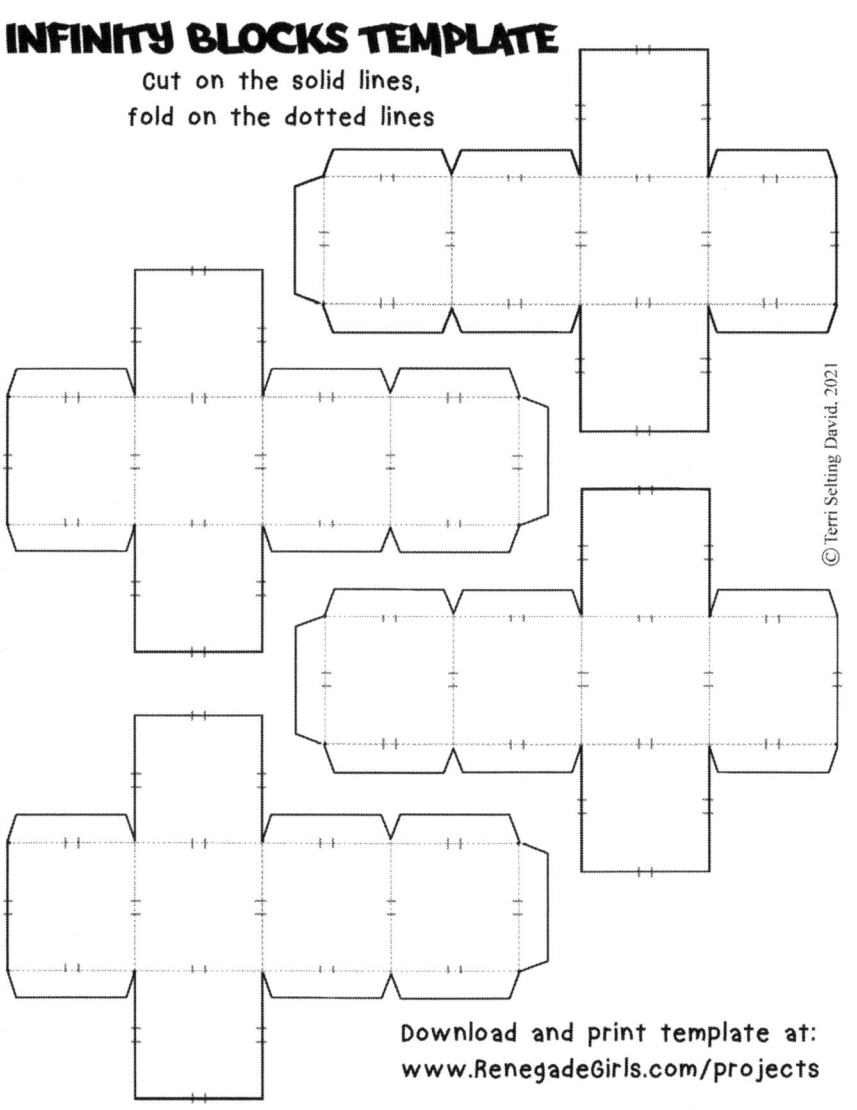

GLOSSARY
KNOW WHAT YOU'RE TALKING ABOUT

A

Aggregate - to collect or mix together the whole entire amount of a bunch of similar things. A beach is an AGGREGATE of grains of sand. A final score is an AGGREGATE of the points earned during a game.

Amp/amperage - an AMP is a standard unit of electrical current, the way a mile is a standard unit of distance or a cup is a standard unit of measuring liquid.

Apparatus - an object used for a certain function.

Aptitude - Your natural ability to do something.

Axle - a shaft attached to the middle of a wheel, used to help the wheel turn.

B

Biography - the true story about someone's life.

Glossary

Brick shot - in basketball, a brick or a brick shot is a really bad shot that had no chance of going in the net.

BuJo/Bullet Journal - a journaling system developed by Ryder Carroll to record anything you want, from to-do lists and calendar items, to doodles or journal entries. The trick is to keep everything in one notebook with an index for easy reference, and consistent symbols for keeping track of tasks.

Button batteries - also called coin cell batteries. Small, round, powerful batteries that look like buttons or quarters, commonly found in cameras, lights, car remotes, and other things. Button batteries can be dangerous if swallowed, so be careful with them!

C

Career - your profession or life's work, usually something specialized that takes practice or special training.

Charge - (electrical) a trait or property that comes from electromagnetic forces. Protons have a positive charge, and electrons have a negative charge. A battery's CHARGE is the amount of potential (available) energy it holds, based on these properties.

Circuit - a path for electricity to move along. The basic components include a power source, a conductive path, a load (something for it to power), and sometimes a switch. There are many other components in a more complex circuit, and most circuits have to be combined with others in order to be useful.

Glossary

Circuit board - a circuit printed on a board, made for connecting electronic components together.

Coin cell batteries - the same as button batteries above.

Components - (electrical) parts of an electrical circuit. They can be single items like transistors, or part of a group of other components.

Conductor, conductive, conductivity - able to transfer something like heat, electricity, or sound from one place to another. Metal is a good conductor, which means electricity can move easily through it. Plastic is a poor conductor (it's an insulator, which is the opposite of a conductor), so electricity doesn't move through it very well.

Conductive thread - sewing thread made out of fibers such as silver, copper, nickel, and stainless steel with a core of cotton or polyester. It carries electricity the same way a wire does, but is flexible enough to sew with.

Corporate/corporation - a business granted the privileges and duties of acting as a separate, single, legal entity.

CPU - a **C**entral **P**rocessing **U**nit is the part of a computer that gets and executes instructions. It is like the brain of a computer.

Current - (electrical) the flow of an electrical charge, like a river is the flow of water.

E

Glossary

Efficient - doing something without wasting resources such as time or energy.

Electricity - a primal force, a force of nature, ELECTRICITY is the flow of particles (electrons and protons) and the energy they make as they move.

Electronics - the study and use of electrical parts and circuits, or a device that uses electricity.

Engineer - someone who solves problems using specialized knowledge. An ENGINEER commonly solves a problem by designing or inventing a solution, whether that solution is an invention, a process, or a system.

Entrepreneur - someone who starts and develops a business. They are the ones who make the decisions, take the risks, have the vision, and enjoy the success or deal with the failure of the business.

H

Hors d'œuvres - food! Little bite-sized snack food served at a party.

I

Input - information, signals, data, or goods that are "put into" something.

Insulate, insulated, insulating - to reduce the flow of electricity or heat energy. A non-conductive material that electricity can't move through, such as rubber, can be used as an insulator to keep the electricity moving only where it should go.

L

Leads (electrical) - the wires coming out of an electrical device that allow electricity to enter and exit the device.

LED - stands for Light Emitting Diode. A device that shines (emits) light.

Leverage - getting mechanical advantage to help influence a situation, like how a lever helps lift something heavy.

M

Motherboard - or *mainboard*. The main circuit board in a complex electronic system, like a computer. It delivers power and communication to and between all the computer's hardware components.

O

Output - information, signals, data, or goods that are produced and "sent out."

Ozone - a pale blue gas with a sharp smell, part of Earth's atmosphere, that is usually produced when a charge of electricity, such as lightning, passes through the air.

P

Parallel circuit - a circuit containing multiple pathways or branches. Each device is on a separate branch and the electricity flowing through the circuit divides to reach

each branch.

Polarity - having two values. In electricity, it means the positive and negative charge, usually shown with a + or -.

Power source - where energy comes from.

R

Resistors - (electrical)an electrical component that limits, or resists, the power of an electrical current to reduce the amount of electricity moving through a circuit.

S

Series circuit - a circuit containing a single pathway through which electricity flows. All the parts of a SERIES CIRCUIT are connected along that same pathway.

Sewn circuit - a working electric circuit sewn onto fabric, usually using conductive thread.

Shaft - a long pole, rod, or handle of something.

Short (Electrical) - a short circuit is an electrical connection between two points electricity is not supposed to go directly between. They can be very dangerous.

Static electricity - the build-up of an electrical charge on the surface of an object.

T

Technology - the use of science to solve problems by inventing new tools or devices.

Trajectory - the path of something moving through

space and time, such as the trail of a thrown ball or the path of an airplane in flight.

V

Volt/voltage - the "push" that causes an electrical charge to move through a wire or other conductor. It's also the unit of measure for that force or push.

ACKNOWLEDGMENTS

Taking this opportunity to send loving thanks, in no particular order, to:

My amazing husband who brings me tea, or wine, depending on the time of day, and believed in me when I didn't, and never complained (out loud) about the light from my laptop late at night.

My son, brilliant and loving, always ready with a cuddle and an ego boost whenever I'm feeling low.

My daughter, my muse, number one fan, original test reader and occasional editor, wise in the ways of tween speech.

My Mom, who spent hours and days and more days editing this book.

All three of my sisters, women in STEM careers, inspiring young girls everywhere as real life rocket scientists, oncologists, and healers.

My Dad, reading through a book written for 9-12 year

old girls countless times and always ready to help wherever he could.

My wonderful In-Laws, my belle-mère and beau-père, for their loving support, feedback, and stepping up to handle the kids and dishes so I could write.

Thanks especially to

Vicky for co-founding Renegade Girls, and being as vibrant and brilliant as you are hard-working. Juliana for writing dates and friendship as well as letting me borrow inspiration from her kids (and thanks to those kids of course!). Briony for inspiration and enthusiastic support. Renee for her love and support. Solène for being such an awesome inspiration and human. And everyone else who has gone on this journey with me.

And I especially want to thank the thousands of Renegade Girls and Boys who've shared their creativity, fun, and amazing tinkering prowess at the Renegade summer camps and after school programs. You are the reason we exist, you are the future. Use your voices and brains and persistence to help each other and save the world!

ABOUT THE AUTHOR

Terri Selting David travelled West in 1996 until she couldn't get any more West. San Francisco stole her heart and allowed her to pursue her love of technology, making stuff, art, and storytelling as a digital character animator. She spent over a decade making video games, film, television, and even comic books. But tech wasn't always the most welcoming place for a woman, no matter how talented and passionate. Once her children came along, she wanted to make the world a better place for them, especially the tech world.

So in 2015, she teamed up with her friend Vicky to found the Renegade Girls Tinkering Club enrichment program to do what she could to make STEM a more welcoming place for the girls of the future. A few years later, she blended her background in storytelling, her digital skills, her art skills, and her experience writing curricula to write the Renegade Girls Tinkering Club novels, to bring her projects to a wider audience and provide positive role models for girls facing the unique challenges of pursuing a love for technology, science, engineering, and math during a fragile time in everyone's life: middle school.

She lives in San Francisco with 2 rowdy children and a fabulous, brilliant husband who brings her tea every night.

ALSO BY TERRI SELTING DAVID

Check out all the adventures of the Renegade Girls at:

www.RenegadeGirls.com

And visit Terri's author website at:

www.TerriSeltingDavid.com

Made in the USA
Columbia, SC
08 January 2022